Fleecie Dolls

Fleecie Dolls

15 adorable toys for children of all ages

Fiona Goble

NEW HOLLAND

First published in 2008 by
New Holland Publishers (UK) Ltd
London • Cape Town • Sydney • Auckland

Garfield House
86-88 Edgware Road
London W2 2EA
United Kingdom
www.newhollandpublishers.com

80 McKenzie Street
Cape Town 8001
South Africa

Level 1, Unit 4
14 Aquatic Drive
Frenchs Forest, NSW 2086
Australia

218 Lake Road
Northcote
Auckland
New Zealand

10 9 8 7 6 5 4 3 2 1

ISBN 978-1-84773-225-5

Editor: Emma Pattison
Design: Roland Codd
Photography: Shona Wood
Production: Jean Pope
Editorial Direction: Rosemary Wilkinson

Reproduction by Colourscan, Singapore
Printed and bound by Craft Print Pte Ltd

Note: Some of the projects in this book are unsuitable for children under
3 years of age due to small parts. Always keep small or sharp objects
(such as needles or buttons) away from small children.

Contents

Introduction

With the detailed instructions in this book, you'll be able to stitch yourself a whole family of gorgeous fleecie dolls in just a few evenings.

There are tiny dolls like Suki who is just 10 cm (4 in) tall and the perfect sized playmate for little hands. And there's cool, leggy Jasmine who stretches right up to 69 cm (27 in) and would feel at home in any girl's bedroom. For the boys, you'll find a monster, an alien and Pedro the pirate – all of them much cuter than the normal varieties, of course.

The dolls are all made from polyester fleece – and that includes their hair and some of their clothes. Fleece is a brilliant fabric because it doesn't slip or fray. It's also very forgiving – so little wobbles won't show. It stretches slightly so you can ease your dolls into the shape you want and your seams will look perfectly smooth. Once you've started making dolls from fleece, I don't think you'll ever want to go back to cotton or calico.

All the dolls are simple to make – with clever techniques and shortcuts replacing the fiddly gussets, facings and tiny buttonholes that used to make sewing cloth dolls so time consuming and tricky.

I hope you enjoy looking through the book and deciding which fleecie dolls you want to make first and how, by choosing your own colour and fabrics, you can make your fleecie dolls unique.

Fiona Goble

Tools & Materials

TOOLS

Before you start making any of the fleecie dolls you will need some basic sewing equipment, some of which you will probably have already and other items you may need to buy.

Photocopier and thin card

The templates on pages 98–110 are shown at 50% of the actual size. The easiest and most accurate way to transfer the templates and enlarge them to 100% is to photocopy the templates onto thin card or thick paper.

Sewing machine and sewing machine needles (1)

You can easily sew the fleecie dolls and clothes by hand but a sewing machine will make it much quicker. All you need is a machine that does basic running stitch, although one that also does zig zag stitch will be useful for giving a professional finish to some of the clothes. Your machine should be fitted with a needle suitable for medium weight fabrics. A standard European size 70 or 80 (US 11 or 12) needle is ideal. It's a good idea to have a few available as machine needles can bend or become blunt quite easily and you will need to replace them fairly often.

Needles for hand sewing (2)

You will need two types of hand sewing needles to make the fleecie dolls – a standard sewing needle and an embroidery needle.

You will need a standard sewing needle (a 'sharp') for hand sewing your fleecie dolls and clothes. Even if you are sewing by machine you will need this type of needle for closing the opening used for stuffing and, for many of the dolls, sewing on features and sewing the feet in position.

To embroider some of the fleecie dolls' features you will also need an embroidery or crewel needle. This is a medium length sharp needle that has an eye large enough for you to thread embroidery thread.

Iron

You will need an iron when making some of the fleecie dolls and their clothes to press open seams, fix bonding web and appliqués, and give a professional finish to some of the finished items.

Water-soluble pen or quilter's pencil (3)

You will need a water-soluble pen or quilter's pencil to draw round the templates and to mark the dolls' features before you sew or embroider them. They work like ordinary pens or pencils but the marks are easily removed by spraying or dabbing with water. The pens usually come in bright blue and are the best option for marking light and medium coloured fabrics. For darker fabrics, choose one of the pencils which come in a range of light colours, including white and yellow. Water-soluble pens and quilter's pencils are widely available in craft and haberdashery shops, and through mail order companies and internet companies that supply accessories for patchwork and quilting.

Ordinary pencil (4)

You will need a pencil for tracing the appliqué shapes featured on some of the clothes onto the backing paper of your bonding web (see page 10). A pencil is sometimes also useful for pushing the toy filling into the dolls' limbs.

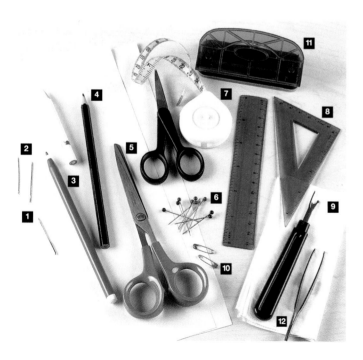

Scissors (5)

Ordinary scissors are fine for cutting your pattern card or paper but you will need a pair of good quality sewing scissors for cutting fabric. You will also need some sharp embroidery scissors for cutting out small items such as the dolls' eyes and cheeks. Make sure that you keep your sewing and embroidery scissors strictly for cutting fabric and threads as using them on card or paper will quickly blunt them.

Dressmaking pins (6)

You will need a small number of dressmaking pins to pin your work together before basting or sewing. It is a good idea to use pins with coloured glass ends. These are much easier to see, and therefore less likely to get left in your work by mistake.

Tape measure (7)

This will be useful for checking the size of your fabric pieces before beginning your project.

Ruler and set square (8)

Some of the projects require you to cut out fabric squares or rectangles of certain sizes, rather than cutting out a template and drawing round it. The quickest and most accurate way of doing this is to use a ruler to draw the sides and a set square to make sure that all the corners are right angles.

Piece of fine cotton (9)

To protect your work, you will need a piece of fine cotton, such as a handkerchief, when ironing the appliqués in position.

Safety pin (10)

You will need a small safety pin to thread the elastic cord through the neck casing and waistbands of some of the fleecie dolls' clothes.

Hole punch (11)

You will need a good quality hole punch to press out some small circles of pink felt for some of the dolls' cheeks.

Stitch ripper and tweezers (12)

These tools will come in handy if you make a mistake and need to undo your work. A stitch ripper has a point on the end and a sharp blade and will enable you to undo stitching without the risk of cutting or pulling the fabric. They are widely available in craft and haberdashery shops. Tweezers are useful for picking out any cut stitches that remain in your work.

MATERIALS

All the materials you need to make the fleecie dolls are available in dress fabric shops and haberdashery stores or from mail order and internet companies. The main fabric used for the dolls themselves is polyester fleece – sometimes called 'polar fleece'. This is the fabric used to make items such as fleece tops, hats and scarves. You will also need polyester toy filling to stuff your fleecie dolls and small quantities of felt and embroidery threads for their features. Depending on which doll you are making, you will also need different fabric for their clothes and accessories and a selection of trimmings. The exact materials needed to make each fleecie doll are given on the individual project pages.

Fleece fabric (1, overleaf)

The dolls, their hair and some of the clothes and accessories are made from polyester fleece fabric. Fleece fabric comes in different thicknesses and finishes. It varies from smooth, thin fabrics used for lightweight tops to thick, shaggy fabrics used for winter jackets. Light and medium fleeces are the ideal fabric for making fleecie dolls as the thicker fabrics are too bulky and difficult to work with.

Fleece fabric has a pile which is often smoother when you stroke it in one direction than any other. It is important when making the dolls, clothes and accessories that the direction of the pile runs down the length of the doll or garment. You will also notice that fleece material is more stretchy when pulled one way than the other. For some of the dolls' hair and a few other items, it is important that the fabric is cut either along the stretch of the fleece or across it. If this is the case, it is mentioned in the text for the individual projects.

Fleece fabric in a good range of colours is available in many dress fabric shops. But don't worry if there isn't a good fabric shop in your area as fleece is also available at competitive prices by mail order or over the internet (see Suppliers page 111).

If you want an even greater choice of colours and textures, you could look at fleece clothing in budget and second hand shops. You could even transform your own old clothes into fleecie dolls!

Polyester filling (2)

This 100 per cent polyester filling is manufactured specially for stuffing soft toys, cushions and other handmade items. It is widely available in craft and haberdashery shops. Always check that the filling you are buying is marked safe and washable and that it conforms to safety standards.

Plain and patterned cottons (3)

For some of the fleecie dolls' clothes you will need small amounts of plain or printed fabrics in 100 per cent cotton or cotton mixes (a blend of polyester and cotton). You don't need to use exactly the same fabric shown in the project, but for patterned fabrics, small to medium size prints usually work best. You can find a good selection in dress fabric shops, craft shops and patchwork shops. There is also a good selection available from mail order and internet companies.

The fabrics and colours you choose will help give your dolls character, so it's worthwhile spending a bit of time selecting a fabric that you really like. Because you only need small quantities, even the more expensive fabrics should be affordable.

Felt (4)

For some of the fleecie dolls' eyes, mouths and cheeks and for a few of the accessories and trimmings, you will need small pieces or scraps of felt. There are two main types of craft felt, both of them widely available and sold in squares measuring about 23 x 23 cm (9 x 9 in) in craft, haberdashery and fabric shops. The first type is made from 100 per cent polyester and the second type is made from a mixture of viscose and wool. I would recommend that you try to find the felt made from viscose and wool because it is slightly thinner than polyester felt and easier to cut into small shapes.

Speciality fabrics (5)

For a small number of fleecie dolls' accessories you will need speciality fabrics such as organza (a thin, shimmery fabric) or metallic fabric.

Polyester wadding or batting (6)

Wadding (sometimes called 'batting') is a light, bulky layer of polyester material, a bit like polyester stuffing, most often used for the middle layer of patchwork quilts. For a couple of fleecie doll accessories you will need a small amount of 7-mm or 8-mm (¼-in) deep polyester wadding. It is available from craft and haberdashery shops and mail order and internet companies selling patchwork and quilting supplies.

Embroidery thread (7)

Some of the fleecie dolls' eyes, noses and mouths are embroidered with 100 per cent cotton stranded embroidery thread. This is made up of six strands that can be easily separated. For the projects in this book you will usually work with three strands. The colour used depends on the doll you are making and the colour of the fleece you are using for the skin colour.

Sewing thread (8)

Whether you are sewing with a machine or by hand, you will need standard sewing threads to match your fabrics. Threads made from 100 per cent polyester, often called 'all purpose', are widely available and come in a very good range of colours.

Elastic cord (9)

For some of the fleecie dolls, you will need narrow elastic cord to thread through the narrow waistbands of the skirts and trousers and the necklines of the dresses. This is widely available and comes in black or white. As it will not usually show, it doesn't really matter which colour you use.

Bonding web (10)

For some of the clothing and accessories you will need a small amount of fusible bonding web to fasten the appliqués. Bonding web is a thin web of dry glue that is fixed on a paper backing. The shape for the appliqué is drawn on the paper backing with a normal pencil. The bonding web is then ironed onto the reverse side of the fabric and cut out. The backing can then be peeled off and the appliqué pressed in place with an iron. There are several brands of bonding web on sale and it is widely available in craft and haberdashery shops.

Seam sealant (11)

Seam sealant is a special type of clear liquid that comes in a small bottle with a pointed nozzle and narrow opening. It is used in some of the projects to prevent material from fraying. It is also useful to prevent ribbon ends from fraying. Although seam sealant is fine to use on most fabrics, test your seam sealant on a scrap of your fabric first. Seam sealant is widely available in craft shops and haberdashery stores.

Fabric glue (12)

Fabric glue is used to apply small pieces of felt in some of the projects. It is usually a special type of PVA glue which is white when you apply it but dries clear. Although fabric glue is fine to use on most fabrics, test your fabric glue on a scrap of your fabric first. Fabric glue is widely available in craft and haberdashery shops.

Trimmings and buttons (13)

For some of the projects you will need buttons, sequins, fabric flowers, ribbons, lace or fancy yarn. You should be able to find a good selection of these in your local craft or haberdashery shop or at internet companies that specialise in fabrics and trimmings. The buttons and trimmings you select are crucial to your project and choosing the right ones will ensure that your fleecie dolls look fantastic. For this reason, it's a good idea to take your time when deciding which ones to use. Shops and internet companies that specialise in card making and scrap booking are a particularly good source of interesting and unusual buttons and ribbons.

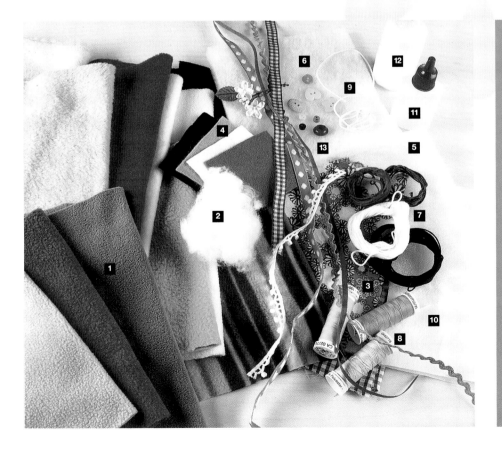

SAFETY

It is very important that you do not give any of the dolls with added extras, such as buttons, to children under three years old as these can be a choking hazard. All of the dolls and their clothes can be easily adapted to suit younger children. For example, the buttons on Daisy the baby doll's dress straps can be omitted and the straps simply hand sewn in place. The button on the blanket could be replaced with a small circle of felt. The button on Jasmine the teen doll's cardigan could be replaced with two short lengths of ribbon and the button on her bag simply omitted.

Techniques

PREPARING YOUR TEMPLATES

All the templates that you need for making the fleecie dolls in this book are on pages 98-110. All templates are shown at 50% of their actual size. The easiest way to prepare your template is to use a photocopier. Simply set the photocopier to enlarge the pieces that you need and photocopy them onto thin card or thick paper and cut them out.

TRANSFERRING YOUR TEMPLATE TO YOUR FABRIC

The easiest way to transfer your pattern is to hold the template firmly in position on the reverse side of your fabric and draw round it using a water-soluble pen or quilter's pencil. You can use the same pen or pencil to mark the positions of the small dots which act as guidelines for sewing and making up your doll. Simply poke the pen nib or pencil tip through the card template or make a hole in the template first using a large needle.

BASIC SEWING SKILLS

If you are sewing your fleecie doll by machine, you will need to use a medium length straight stitch to sew your doll together and to stitch the clothes. Some of the clothes also recommend a zig zag stitch round some of the raw edges, although this is optional.

If you are sewing by hand, use a standard 'sharps' sewing needle and a small running stitch. Work a small back stitch every few stitches for extra strength.

To secure your work at the beginning and end, work a few stitches on top of each other if you are sewing by hand. If you are using a sewing machine, most machines have a reverse direction so you can sew a short length of reverse stitching before you begin and after you complete your sewing to secure the stitches in place.

Basting

Because fleece is not a slippery fabric, most of the fleecie dolls can be completed by simply pinning the pieces of work together before sewing. For some of the steps in some of the projects, however, it is easier if you baste your fabric first. Basting stitches are temporary stitches that are pulled out after your work is finished. They are large running stitches and, so long as they are holding your work in position securely, they do not have to be particularly even or tidy. It is sensible to baste in a contrasting thread colour so that you can easily tell which thread to pull out.

Stuffing and closing openings

Always use a small amount of toy filling at a time when you are stuffing your dolls. Also, try not to push each bit in too hard or your doll will look lumpy. The dolls should look fully stuffed but have a nice squashy feel. You can push the stuffing into the dolls using the blunt end of a pencil or something similar – but make sure that you don't use anything too sharp or push too hard or you might break the stitching.

Once your fleecie doll has been turned the right way out and you are pleased with the way it looks, you will need to close the opening that you have used for stuffing. The neatest way is to slip stitch the two edges together. Fold in the raw edges of both sides of the opening, in line with the seam line. From the inside, bring your needle out through

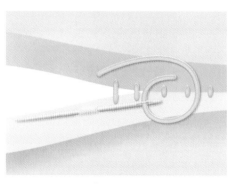

Slip stitch

Oversewing

one side of the fold at the beginning of the opening. Take the needle in through the fold directly opposite and out through the same fold, about 3 mm (⅛ in) further up. Work a few stitches at a time before pulling your thread taut.

Oversewing

This stitch is used to fasten some of the felt and fleece features to the heads of the dolls. It is also useful for joining sections of some of the dolls together. Use small stitches to make evenly spaced stitches along the fabric edge or across two pieces of fabric. In the case of felt features, use the point of a fine needle to gently tease the fabric round the stitches so that they become virtually invisible.

Gathering

One of the projects requires the fabric to be gathered before it is sewn in place. If you are using a sewing machine, set your machine to a large stitch size and work two rows of stitching along the edge to be gathered. The first row should be about 4 mm (⅛-¼ in) from the edge and the second about 2 mm (½ in) from the edge. Do not reverse stitch to secure at either end and leave a 'tail' of about 5 cm (2 in) at each end. Pull up the gathered stitches by pulling on the two tails at one edge of the fabric and arrange the gathers evenly across the fabric. If you are sewing by hand, work two rows of medium size hand running stitch and gather your fabric in the same way. Once you have stitched the gathered fabric in place, you can pull out the gathering stitches. For this reason, you might like to sew them in a contrasting thread so you can see exactly where they are.

Hemming stitch

If you are using a sewing machine, you can use a small zig zag stitch or a normal straight stitch to hem the dolls' dresses or skirts. If you are sewing by hand, it is best to use a hemming stitch. This is a bit like slip stitch. Begin by fastening your thread to the folded hem allowance. Pick up a thread or two of the garment using the point of your needle. Then take your needle back into the folded edge of the hem and out again 5 or 6 mm (¼ in) further along, ready for the next stitch.

SPECIAL EMBROIDERY STITCHES

For some of the fleecie dolls you will need to use special embroidery stitches. Instructions for these stitches are given below.

Back stitch (see diagram overleaf)

This is used to work the mouths of many of the dolls. To work a row of back stitch, bring your thread out at your starting point and start by working a single running stitch. Insert your needle back into the end point of the first stitch then out again, a little further on from the end of the last stitch.

Chain stitch (see diagrams overleaf)

This is used for the mouth of some of the dolls. For chain stitch, bring your needle out at the point where you want your chain to start. Insert the needle back into the same hole and out at the point you want the stitch to end – about 3 mm (⅛ in) further on – making sure your thread is under the needle point (step 1). Now pull the thread through. You

Gathering

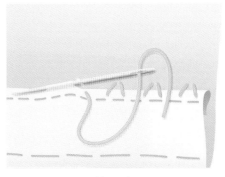

Hemming

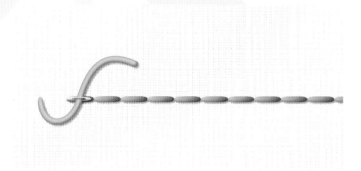

Back stitch

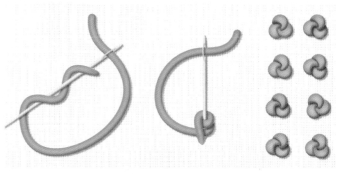

French knot

are now ready to start the second stitch (step 2). At the end of the row, make a small stitch over the last loop to hold it in position (step 3).

French knot

This is used for the eyes of a small number of dolls. To make a French knot, bring your needle out in the position where you want the knot to be. Wind your thread twice round the needle as shown in the diagram, keeping the needle as close as you can to the fabric. Insert the point of the needle back through the fabric, just by your starting point. Now gently push the threads down the needle and pull you thread through.

Lazy daisy stitch (see diagrams on page 15)

This is used for the eyes of one of the dolls. A lazy daisy stitch is really a group of single chain stitches. To work a lazy daisy stitch, bring your thread out at the point where

you want the base of the stitch. Insert your needle back into this point and out again at the point where you want the tip of the stitch, making sure your thread is under the needle point (step 1). Now pull the thread through. Insert your needle over the chain loop to secure it, and bring it out at the starting point of your next stitch (step 2). Repeat to make a daisy shape (step 3).

Blanket stitch (see diagrams on page 15)

This is used around the blanket accessory of one of the dolls. (Note: These instructions are for working blanket stitch around the outside of a hemmed piece of fabric, as required for the project.)

To begin, take your needle out at your starting point at the folded edge of your work. (The easiest way to do this is to tie a knot at the bottom of your thread and to conceal the knot just under the raw edge of the base of the hem.) Insert your needle back through your fabric, a stitch width

Chain stitch

Step 1

Step 2

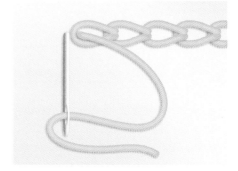

Step 3

Lazy daisy stitch

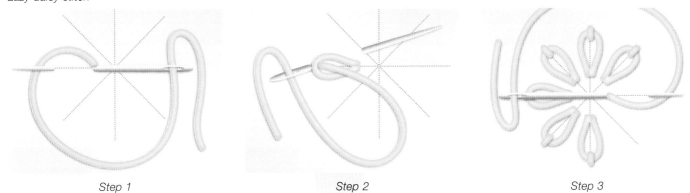

| Step 1 | Step 2 | Step 3 |

to the side. Now bring the needle round the back of the folded edge, directly above this point (**step 1**). Make sure your thread is under the needle point and pull up gently to make your first stitch (step 2). Work round the folded edge in the same way, taking care to make your stitches the same height and width (step 3). To blanket stitch round a corner, work in the same way but take your needle up through the middle of the fabric at the corner and out of the centre point, instead of round the outside.

BEGINNING AND FINISHING YOUR STITCHING

When you are embroidering your dolls' features, the neatest way to conceal your thread at the beginning and end of your work is to make a couple of tiny stitches in the seam. You can do this underneath the hair or on a part of the doll that will be concealed by clothes. The stitches should be barely noticeable. When you are stitching felt or fleece features, you can work a couple of tiny stitches on the outside of your work as, like the other stitches, they will 'sink' into the fabric and will be virtually invisible on the finished doll.

A NOTE ON MEASUREMENTS

All the measurements in this book are given in metric units (millimetres or centimetres) with the measurement in inches and fractions of an inch given in brackets afterwards. It is difficult to convert small measurements exactly so figures have been rounded up or down, usually to the nearest ¼ in. In some cases, the measurements are given as 'between ¼ and ½ in'. Because the conversions are not exact, it is important that you follow one system only rather than mix the two.

Blanket stitch

| Step 1 | Step 2 | Step 3 |

FLORENCE *The traditional cloth doll*

Sweet natured and traditional in her Mary Jane shoes, Florence is based on the first fleecie doll I ever made. Once you've seen the great results you can achieve when sewing in fleece, I don't think you'll want to make cloth dolls in cotton or calico ever again. Dolls like Florence are so much softer and cosier and make the perfect playmates for little girls everywhere.

You will need

MATERIALS
For the doll
- A piece of cream fleece, measuring 30 x 60 cm (12 x 24 in)
- 2 pieces of bright yellow fleece, each measuring 12 x 9 cm (4¾ x 3½ in) for hair (this should be cut so that the stretch of the fabric lies along the longer length of the fabric)
- Scrap of dark grey felt for the eyes
- Scrap of pale pink fleece or felt for the cheeks
- Red embroidery thread for the mouth
- 40 g (1½ oz) of polyester toy filling
- Matching threads for the cream fleece, pale pink fleece and dark grey felt

For the clothes, shoes and hair decoration
- 2 pieces of bright pink fleece, each measuring 20 x 24 cm (8 x 9½ in) for the dress (if fleece has an obvious pile, this should run down the longer length of the fabric)

- A 36-cm (14-in) length of pale blue ric rac braid for the dress
- 2 medium size white buttons for the dress
- A piece of dark grey fleece, measuring 7 x 28 cm (2¾ x 11 in) for the shoes (if the fleece has an obvious pile, this should run down the shorter length of the fabric)
- 2 small white buttons for the 'buckles' on the shoes
- Matching threads for all your fabrics and for the ric rac braid
- A scrap of turquoise fleece for the hair accessory
- A small button for the hair accessory

TOOLS
- Access to a photocopier
- Scissors
- Dressmaking pins
- Water-soluble pen or quilter's pencil
- Sewing machine (optional)
- Sewing needles

Florence is approximately 38 cm (15 in) tall

To make the doll

1 Photocopy the head and body, arm and leg templates on page 98. Cut out two head and body pieces, four arm and four leg pieces. For the arm pieces, cut two shapes using the template the right way up and two pieces using it face down. Make sure that any obvious pile on the fleece runs down the length of the body pieces and remember to mark the position of the small dots.

2 Fold one of the head and body pieces in half lengthwise, right sides together and sew the shaping dart on the head using a small running stitch or medium length machine stitch. Seam the arm pieces to the top of the two body pieces, allowing a 5-mm (¼-in) seam allowance and matching the small dots. Make sure that the thumbs are uppermost.

3 With the right sides of the two head and body pieces together, seam down each side of the doll, from the small dots at the side of the face to the waist, leaving a 5-mm (¼-in) seam allowance and leaving the top of the head open. Make a small snip into the seam at the neck curves to prevent any puckering. Now turn your work right sides out.

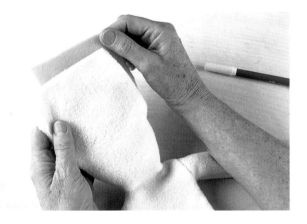

4 Place your two pieces of yellow fleece right sides together and insert into the opening at the top of the head so that the shorter edge comes just below the small dots at the side of the head. Secure in place with a pin. Sew along the curve at the top of the head, as shown on your template, using a small running stitch or medium length machine stitch. You may find it useful to draw your sewing line with the water-soluble pen or quilter's pencil.

5 Make the doll's legs by placing two leg pieces right sides together. Seam around the leg, allowing a 5-mm (¼-in) seam allowance and leaving the top end open for stuffing. Turn the legs the right way out and stuff them.

6 Stuff the doll's head, body and arms, easing them into shape as you go. Turn under 5 mm (¼ in) along lower edge of body and baste. Insert the legs into the opening, so that the outer side seams of the legs are in line with the outer edge of the body. Slip stitch in place using your thread double for extra strength and slip stitch across crotch.

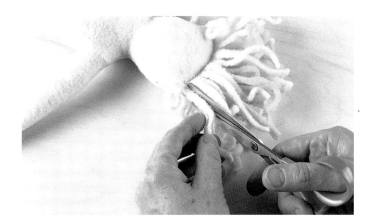

7 For the hair, cut into the cream and yellow hair sections, from the tip almost to the root. The strips should be about 3 mm (⅛ in) wide. To make the hair curly, stretch each strip separately to its full length and then let it fall back in place.

8 Cut out two eyes from the dark grey felt and two cheeks from the pale pink fleece or felt. Using the photograph as a guide, position the eyes and cheeks and oversew them in place. If you are using felt for the cheeks, gently tease round the stitches with the tip of a needle. Work the mouth in back stitch using three strands of red embroidery thread. Work large running stitches over the eyes so that the stitches form a star shape.

To make the dress

1 Photocopy the dress and pocket templates on page 98 and cut them out. Use the templates to cut out two dress shapes and two pocket shapes from the bright pink fleece, making sure any pile runs down the length of the dress. Position the pockets on the front of the dress as shown on the template and sew round the sides and bottom of the pockets, close to the edge, using a small running stitch or medium length machine stitch.

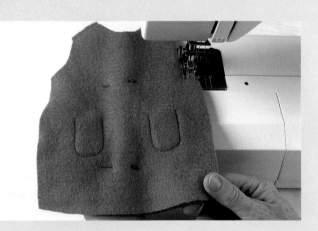

2 Place the two dress shapes right sides together and seam at the shoulders and sides using a small running stitch or medium length machine stitch. Trim the shoulder seams slightly to give a neater finish. If you are using a sewing machine that has zig zag stitch, work a row of small zig zag stitches round the hem of the dress, stretching it slightly as you go. This is not essential but will give you a professional looking finish.

3 Turn the dress the right way out. Place the ric rac braid around the edge of the dress about 2.5 cm (1 in) up from the lower edge. Stitch in place along the centre of the braid using matching thread. To complete the dress, sew the two buttons in position, using the photograph as a guide.

To make the shoes

1 Photocopy the shoe template on page 98 and cut it out. Use the template to cut out four shoe shapes from the dark grey fleece. Make sure any obvious pile on the fleece runs down the length of the shoe shapes. Mark the shoe fronts, as shown on the template, on the reverse side of two of the pieces of fleece, using a water-soluble pen or quilter's pencil.

2 Without cutting out the hole on the shoe fronts, work a small running stitch or medium machine stitch round the entire edge of the area. Once you have done this, cut the hole out carefully, close to the stitching, using embroidery scissors.

To make the hair accessory

Cut out a flower shape from a scrap of turquoise fleece. Sew the button in place for the flower centre and stitch the flower in place in Florence's hair.

3 Place each shoe front on a shoe back so that the right sides of the fabric are together and seam around the sides, allowing a 5-mm (¼-in) seam allowance and leaving the top open. Trim the seams closely. Turn the right way out and sew on small button 'buckles' at the outside edge of each shoe, as shown in the photograph.

Good idea For a different outfit for Florence, make a short version of the dress to create a tunic top and use a rectangle of a favourite cotton fabric to create a simple skirt.

ABBIE & ALFIE The comforter dolls

These soft creatures are a cross between a doll and a security blanket and would make a perfect gift for a newborn baby. The head and hands are lightly stuffed but the body is left unstuffed so the dolls have a lovely floppy feel. I have made these dolls in traditional pastel shades but they would work just as well in something bright and funky.

You will need

MATERIALS

- 2 pieces of pale pink or pale blue fleece, each measuring approximately 35 x 30 cm (14 x 12 in) (if the fleece has an obvious pile, this should run down the longer length of the fabric)
- 1 small piece of cream fleece for the face
- 1 small piece of bright pink or bright blue fleece for the heart appliqué
- A scrap of mid-pink fleece or felt for the cheeks
- Dark grey and red embroidery threads
- A piece of bonding web
- 15 g (½ oz) of polyester toy filling
- Matching threads for all your fabrics

TOOLS

- Access to a photocopier
- Pencil
- Scissors
- Dressmaking pins
- Water-soluble pen or quilter's pencil
- Sewing machine (optional)
- Sewing needles
- Iron
- A piece of fine cotton such as a handkerchief to protect the appliqué when fixing with the iron

Abbie and Alfie are approximately 30 cm (12 in) long

To make the dolls

1 Photocopy the body and cheek templates on page 99 and cut them out. Place the body template onto the reverse of one piece of pastel fleece, making sure that any obvious pile runs down the length of the body shape. Draw round the template with the water-soluble pen or quilter's pencil, remembering to mark the small dots. Now cut the shape out. Remember, you only need to cut out one body shape at this stage.

2 To make the face, photocopy the face template on page 99 and trace onto the backing paper of a piece of bonding web, using an ordinary pencil. Next, with the iron on a warm setting, iron the bonding web onto the reverse of the piece of cream fleece. Cut the shape out carefully.

3 Peel off the backing paper of the bonding web and place the face in the position shown on the template, with the top of the head butting up to the line shown on the template and the face in the centre of the head. Make sure that any obvious pile runs down the length of the face. Place a piece of fine cotton, such as a cotton handkerchief, over the face to protect it and iron the face in position. Secure the face by working a small machine zig zag stitch all round it, or oversew it by hand.

4 To make the heart appliqué, photocopy the heart template on page 99 and trace onto the backing paper of a piece of bonding web. Iron the bonding web onto the reverse of the small piece of bright fleece, making sure that any obvious pile runs down the length of the heart. Cut the heart out carefully and iron it in position using the technique described in step 3. Machine or hand stitch round the heart about 3 mm (⅛ in) from the edge.

5 Mark the position for the eyes, as shown on the template. Using three strands of dark grey embroidery thread, embroider the eyes using lazy daisy stitch (see page 14). Using three strands of red embroidery thread, embroider the mouth using back stitch.

6 Use the cheek templates to cut out two cheeks from the mid-pink fleece or felt. Place the cheeks in position, as shown on the template, and oversew them in place. If you are using felt for the cheeks, gently tease round the stitches with the tip of a needle, so that the stitches become almost invisible. (If you use fleece for the cheeks, you do not need to do this.)

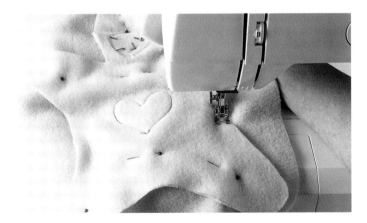

7 Now place your second piece of pastel fleece face up on a hard surface, making sure any obvious pile runs down the length of the fabric. Place the doll front face down on the second piece of fleece and pin or baste it in place. Now sew around the entire outside of the doll, allowing a 5-mm (¼-in) seam allowance, leaving an opening for stuffing, as shown on the template. Trim the excess fabric to match the doll shape.

8 Turn the doll the right way out and stuff the head lightly and the hands slightly more firmly. To secure the stuffing in the head, using your thread double, work a curved row of hand running stitch about 1 cm (⅜ in) below the lower edge of the face, as shown on the template. To secure the stuffing in the hands, work a line of running stitch around the wrists using your thread double. Pull the thread up slightly to form a wrist, and secure. Now close the opening used for stuffing using slip stitch.

LIZZIE & NINA The folk dolls

Lizzie's and Nina's ancestors are the beautifully simple Shaker folk dolls of America. They are made from just two pieces of fleece and their dresses are made from two rectangles of cotton – so they are one of the very easiest dolls to make in the book and an ideal project for beginners. They are made in exactly the same way, apart from their hair.

You will need

MATERIALS
For the doll
- 2 pieces of cream or mid-brown fleece, each measuring approximately 29 x 26 cm (11½ x 10¼ in) (if the fleece has an obvious pile, this should run down the longer length of the fabric)
- A piece of yellow fleece measuring 18 x 2 cm (7 x ¾ in) (if the fleece stretches in one direction only, it should stretch along the length of the fabric) or a scrap of black fleece
- A scrap of mid-pink felt for the cheeks (Lizzie only)
- Fabric glue for applying the cheeks (Lizzie only)
- Black and red embroidery threads
- 20 g (¾ oz) of polyester toy filling
- Matching thread for your fabrics

For the clothes and hair accessories
- 2 pieces of thin printed cotton fabric, each measuring 22 x 14 cm (8¾ x 5½ in) (it is important that the fabric is quite thin so that the gathers round the neck do not look too bulky)

Lizzie and Nina are approximately 25 cm (10 in) tall

- 15 cm (6in) of elastic cord
- 1 small co-ordinating button
- matching thread
- 50 cm (20 in) of 5-mm (¼-in) wide ribbon for Lizzie's plaits

TOOLS
- Access to a photocopier
- Scissors
- Dressmaking pins
- Water-soluble pen or quilter's pencil
- Sewing machine (optional)
- Sewing needles
- Iron
- Small safety pin for threading the elastic cord
- Hole punch (Lizzie only)

To make the dolls

1 Photocopy the doll template on page 100 and cut it out. Place the body template onto the reverse of one piece of fleece, making sure that any obvious pile runs down the length of the body shape. Draw round the template with the water-soluble pen or quilter's pencil, remembering to mark the small dots. Now cut the shape out. Remember, you only need to cut out one body shape at this stage.

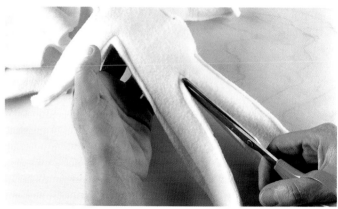

2 Lay the doll front face down on the second piece of fleece and sew around the outside, allowing a 5-mm (¼-in) seam allowance and leaving an opening for stuffing. Trim away the excess fabric on the second piece of fleece to match the doll shape. Snip the seam allowance at the doll's crotch to help prevent any puckering round the crotch. Turn the doll the right way out through the opening and stuff. Close the opening used for stuffing using slip stitch.

3 To make Lizzie's hair, cut the yellow fleece into three even strips. Secure the strips at the centre of the head and again half way down each side. Plait the strips each side and secure the plaits by tying two of the ends together in a single knot. To make Nina's hair, cut the black fleece into five thin strips. Sew the centre point of each strip to the centre seam of the head so the strips are evenly spaced across the top of the head.

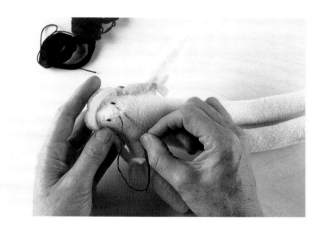

4 Mark the position of the eyes and mouth using the water-soluble pen or quilter's pencil. For the eyes, with three strands of black embroidery thread, work two or three 3-mm (⅛-in) stitches in and out of the same holes or use French knots (see page 14). For the mouth, using three strands of red embroidery thread, work two small stitches in a V-shape. For Lizzie, use the hole punch to press out two circles from the mid-pink felt and glue in position.

To make the dress

1 Lay the two rectangles of printed cotton fabric right sides together. Measure down 7 cm (2¾ in) from the top of the fabric on each side and make a small mark with the water-soluble pen or quilter's pencil on the reverse of your fabric. This will mark the bottom of the armholes. Seam down each side from the bottom of the armhole to the bottom of the dress, leaving a 5-mm (¼-in) seam allowance.

2 Press under 5 mm (¼ in) on each side of the armholes and press open the side seams using the iron. If you are using a sewing machine, work a small zig zag stitch down the raw edges on both sides of the armholes. If you are hand stitching, tuck under the raw edge of the armholes and slip stitch in place.

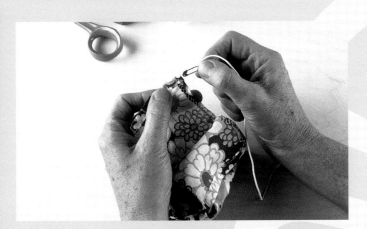

3 Press under 5 mm (¼ in) along the top edges of both sides of the dress. Press under another 5 mm (¼ in) to form a casing and stitch very close to the folded edge. Using the small safety pin, thread the elastic through the casing. Pull up the elastic quite tightly (so the neck of the dress is about the same width as the doll's neck) and knot the ends together. Trim the knot ends and conceal the knot in the casing.

4 Press under 5 mm (¼ in) along the bottom edge of the dress. Press under another 5 mm (¼ in) and stitch close to the folded edge, using a small zig zag stitch if sewing by machine or a hand hemming stitch. To finish the doll, sew the button at the centre of the neck edge and, for Lizzie, tie a length of ribbon round the end of each plait.

SUKI & FRIENDS Sweet and simple dolls

These tiny dolls are inspired by the traditional Kokeshi dolls from Japan which are made from wood. This trio, of course, is made from fleece. Suki, the original sweet and simple doll I made, now has a couple of friends – Joseph and Maya. The beauty of these dolls lies not just in their simplicity but in the fact that by changing the colour of their outfit and the decorations, they are almost infinitely adaptable.

You will need

MATERIALS

For the dolls

- A piece of cream, beige or light brown fleece measuring approximately 14 x 19 cm (5½ x 7½ in) (if the fleece has an obvious pile, this should run down the longer length of the fabric)
- Matching thread
- Dark grey and red embroidery threads
- 15 g (½ oz) of polyester toy filling for each doll

For the hair, clothes and accessories

For Suki

- A piece of purple fleece measuring approximately 11 x 14 cm (4½ x 5½ in) (if the fleece has an obvious pile this should run down the shorter length of the fabric)
- A small piece of black fleece for the hair
- A small piece of yellow fleece and a small piece of bonding web for the flower appliqué
- A red button for the flower centre
- A 15-cm (6-in) length of 3-mm (⅛-in) wide cream ribbon for the hair bow

For Joseph

- A piece of lime green fleece measuring approximately 11 x 14 cm (4½ x 5½ in) (if the fleece has an obvious pile this should run down the shorter length of the fabric)
- A small piece of red fleece for the hat
- Three heart-shaped buttons in assorted colours and sizes to decorate the jumper

For Maya

- A piece of pale pink fleece measuring approximately 11 x 14 cm (4½ x 5½ in) (if the fleece has an obvious pile this should run down the shorter length of the fabric)
- A small piece of yellow fleece for the hair
- A cream heart-shaped button to decorate the jumper
- A 25-cm (10-in) length of 1-cm (⅜-in) wide red gingham ribbon for the hair bow

Suki and friends are approximately 10 cm (4 in) tall

TOOLS

- Access to a photocopier
- Pencil (Suki only)
- Scissors
- Dressmaking pins
- Water-soluble pen or quilter's pencil
- Sewing machine (optional)
- Sewing needles
- Iron (Suki only)
- A piece of fine cotton such as a handkerchief to protect the appliqué when fixing with the iron (Suki only)

For each doll's outfit, you will also need matching threads for all your fabrics

To make the dolls

1 Photocopy the doll template on page 100 and cut it out. Place the piece of fleece for the body face down on a hard, flat surface. Place the template onto the fleece, making sure that any obvious pile runs down the length of the body shape. Pin the template to the fleece or hold it firmly in place and draw round the template with the water-soluble pen or quilter's pencil, remembering to mark the small dots. Now cut the shape out.

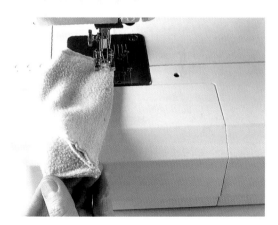

2 Fold the top triangle of the doll piece over to one side so that the tip of the triangle meets the corner of the side edge. Starting at the inner edge (near the base of the triangle), sew the triangle side to the top edge of the body, leaving a 5-mm (¼ in) seam allowance, and stopping 5 mm (¼ in) from the edge. Sew the other side of the triangle to the second edge of the body in exactly the same way. Make the base of the doll in exactly the same way.

3 Sew the back seam of the doll, allowing a 5-mm (¼-in) seam allowance and leaving an opening between the two dots for stuffing. Turn the doll the right way out and stuff firmly. Your doll will stand more steadily if you stuff the head end quite lightly and the base end more firmly. Slip stitch the opening closed.

4 To make the neck, using your thread double and starting at the back seam, run a line of running stitch round the doll, starting 3.5 cm (1¼-1½ in) down from the top of the head. Pull your thread up slightly and secure.

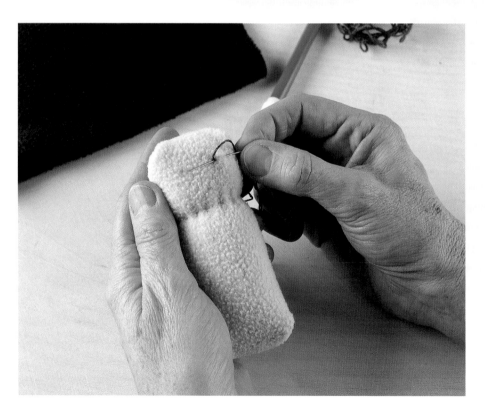

5 Mark the position of the eyes and mouth using the water-soluble pen or quilter's pencil, using the photograph as a guide. For Suki's eyes, using three strands of dark grey embroidery thread, work two slightly slanted 5-mm (¼-in) stitches in and out of the same holes. For Joseph's and Maya's eyes, using three strands of dark grey embroidery, work three 5-mm (¼-in) vertical stitches in and out of the same holes. With three strands of red embroidery thread, make the mouth by working two 5-mm (¼-in) small horizontal stitches in and out of the same holes.

To make the clothes and hair

1 Prepare the jumper template on page 100 in the same way as the body template and cut out the jumper shape, making sure that any obvious pile runs down the shorter length of the shape.

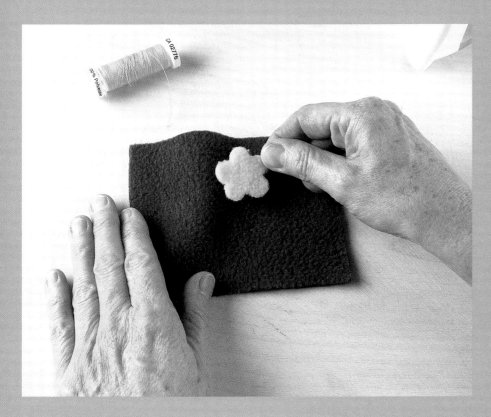

2 Photocopy the flower template on page 100 and trace onto the backing paper of a piece of bonding web, using an ordinary pencil. Next, with the iron on a warm setting, iron the bonding web onto the reverse of the piece of yellow fleece then cut the flower out. Peel off the backing paper of the bonding web and place the flower in the position shown on the jumper template, remembering that any obvious pile on your fabric is running down the jumper. Place the piece of fine cotton over the flower and iron it in position. Work a machine or hand running stitch round the petal edges. Sew the red button in the centre.

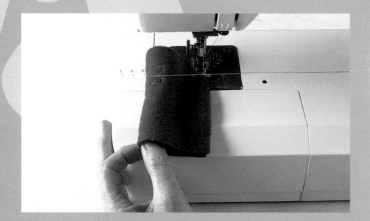

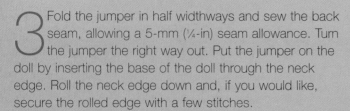

3 Fold the jumper in half widthways and sew the back seam, allowing a 5-mm (¼-in) seam allowance. Turn the jumper the right way out. Put the jumper on the doll by inserting the base of the doll through the neck edge. Roll the neck edge down and, if you would like, secure the rolled edge with a few stitches.

4 Prepare the hair template on page 100 in the same way as the body template and cut out the hair shape from the black fleece. With right sides of the fabric together, hand stitch the sides of the fringe to the side of the hair, allowing a 3-mm (⅛-in) seam allowance. Now hand stitch the two sides of the hair together at the back, again allowing a 3-mm (⅛-in) seam allowance. Turn the hair the right way out and secure to the head with a few stitches. Tie the bow and secure in the hair with a couple of stitches.

JOSEPH

Using lime green fleece, make the jumper in exactly the same way as for Suki, omitting the flower decoration and adding three coloured heart-shaped buttons.

Make Joseph's hat by preparing the hat template on page 100 in the normal way. Cut out the hat from red fleece, making sure that the longer length of the hat shape runs along the less stretchy part of the fleece (this may mean that the pile of the fleece does not run down the length of the finished hat but will ensure a much better fit). Fold the hat shape in half widthways and seam down the shorter side, allowing a 5-mm (¼-in) seam allowance. Using your thread double, run a line of running stitch round the top of the hat. Pull up your thread tightly and secure and turn the hat the right way out.

MAYA

Using pale pink fleece, make Maya's jumper in exactly the same way as for Suki, omitting the flower decoration and adding a cream heart-shaped button. Make Maya's hair in the same way as for Suki and decorate it with a bow made from the red gingham ribbon.

Good idea To create a cute snowman, make a sweet simple doll in pure white fleece. A hat like Joseph's, a fabric scrap scarf and a few buttons will transform your doll into a gorgeous little snowman.

POPPY flower fairy

Flower fairies are dressed in clothes to match the wild flowers they care for. They are among the most adorable of all fairies and Poppy is no exception. She is made from just two pieces of fleece and her 'dress' – actually a skirt and top – is much easier to make than it looks. She would be the perfect gift for any young girl who loves fairies and all things magical.

You will need

MATERIALS
For the doll
- 2 pieces of cream fleece, each measuring approximately 22 x 28 cm (8¾ x 11 in) (if the fleece has an obvious pile, this should run down the longer length of the fabric)
- A piece of yellow fleece for the hair, measuring approximately 6 x 24 cm (2½ x 9½ in) (the length of the fabric should run along the most stretchy part of the fleece)
- A scrap of pale pink fleece or felt for the cheeks
- Dark grey embroidery thread
- 20 g (¾ oz) of polyester toy filling
- Matching threads for all your fabrics

For the clothes and wings
- A piece of red cotton or cotton mix fabric, measuring approximately 14 x 32 cm (5½ x 12½ in)
- A small piece of red fleece for the bodice
- A small piece of lime green fleece for the sepal trim
- 2 pieces of pale pink organza fabric, each measuring approximately 22 x 10 cm (8¾ x 4 in)
- A piece of thin wadding or batting measuring approximately 22 x 10 cm (8¾ x 4 in) for the wings
- matching threads for all your fabrics
- A 20-cm (8-in) length of elastic cord
- A 50-cm (20-in) length of 13-mm (½-in) wide green organza ribbon
- A small fabric flower
- Yellow embroidery thread (for fastening the flower)
- Liquid seam sealant (to prevent ribbons, wings and skirt fabric from fraying)

TOOLS
- Access to a photocopier
- Scissors
- Dressmaking pins
- Small safety pin for threading the elastic cord
- Water-soluble pen or quilter's pencil
- Sewing machine (optional)
- Sewing needles
- Iron

Poppy is approximately 21 cm (8¼ in) tall

To make the doll

1 Photocopy the doll template on page 101 and cut it out. Place one piece of the cream fleece face down on a hard, flat surface. Place the doll template onto the fleece, making sure that any obvious pile runs down the length of the body shape. Pin the template to the fleece or hold it firmly in place and draw round the template with the water-soluble pen or quilter's pencil, remembering to mark the position of the small dots. Now cut the shape out. Remember, you only need to cut out one body shape at this stage.

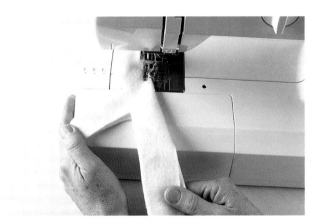

2 Fold the body piece in half lengthways so that the fleecie side of the fabric is on the inside. Sew the body dart – from the centre of the face into the neck, then from the neck outwards to the tummy – using a small running stitch or medium length machine stitch. Now place your second piece of fleece face up on a hard surface, making sure any obvious pile runs down the length of the fabric. Lay the doll shape face down on the second piece of fleece and pin or baste in place.

3 Sew around the outside of the doll, allowing a 5-mm (¼-in) seam allowance, leaving an opening for stuffing, as shown on the template. Trim away the excess fabric on the second piece of fleece to match the doll shape, taking care not to cut through the stitching. Make a snip in the seam allowance at the doll's crotch – this will help prevent any puckering. Turn the doll the right way out through the opening and stuff. Slip stitch the opening closed.

4 To shape the feet, turn up 3 cm (1¼ in) at the end of each leg and hold in place so that the foot is at a right angle to the leg. Now, using the thread double for strength and starting at one of the side seams, work a few large, loose slip stitches across the curve at the front of the ankle. Pull up the thread fairly tightly and secure.

5 To make the hair cut into the fleece every 5 mm (¼ in) across the two shorter edges, stopping just short of the centre. Position the hair across the head so that the hair begins about 1.5 cm (¾ in) below the seam at the top of the head, on the dolls forehead. Secure the hair in place by back stitching along the centre parting. Mark the position of the eyes, mouth and cheeks with the water-soluble pen or quilter's pencil. For the eyes, with three strands of dark grey embroidery thread, work three or four 7-mm (¼-in) vertical stitches in an out of the same holes. Work the mouth in back stitch. Cut out two cheeks from the pale pink fleece or felt. Place the cheeks in position and oversew them in place.

To make the dress

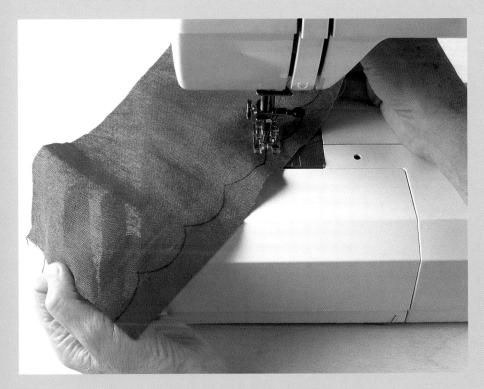

1 Photocopy the skirt, bodice and sepal trim templates on page 101 and cut them out. For the skirt template, first cut the complete rectangle shape. Place the skirt template onto the red cotton or polycotton. Pin the template to the fabric or hold firmly, draw round the template and cut it out. Now cut the scallop shaping on the template and place it on the skirt piece. Using the water-soluble pen or quilter's pencil, now mark the scallop shaping but do not cut it out. Sew a line of machine stitching or hand running stitch along the scallop line. Trim carefully about 2 mm (¹⁄₁₂ in) to the outside of the stitching. Run a thin line of liquid seam sealant round the scalloped edge and leave to dry.

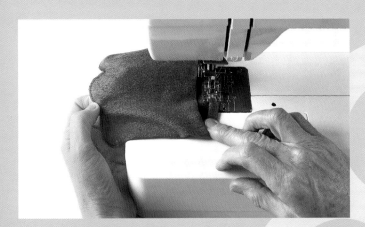

2 Fold the skirt in half and sew the back seam, leaving a 5-mm (¼-in) seam allowance. Turn down 1 cm (⅜ in) at the top of the skirt and press in place with the iron. Turn down another 1 cm (⅜ in) and press again. Stitch as close as possible to the folded edge, leaving a 1-cm (⅜-in) opening at the back. Using the small safety pin, thread the elastic cord through the waistband casing. Pull the elastic up then knot the ends of the elastic together tightly and trim.

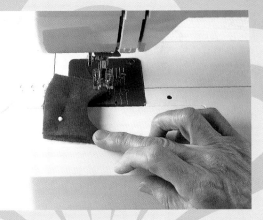

3 Using the bodice template, cut out two bodices from the red fleece, making sure that any pile on your fabric runs down the length of the bodice and marking the small dots to indicate the lower edge of the armholes. Place the two bodice pieces right sides together and sew shoulder seams, allowing a 5-mm (¼-in) seam allowance. Trim the seam allowance close to the stitching.

To make the wings

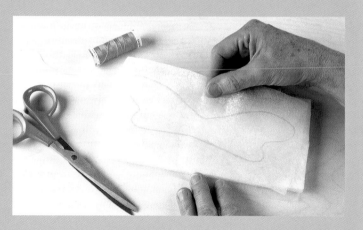

4 Cut out two sepal trims from the lime green fleece, making sure that the pile runs down the length of the fleece from the straight part to the pointed edges and marking the position of the small dots. Place a sepal trim on the bodice, so that the top of the sepal trim slightly overlaps the lower edge of the bodice and baste in place. Fasten the sepal trim to the bodice using a machine zig zag stitch or oversew by hand.

1 Photocopy the wing template on page 101 and cut it out. Place the wing template on one of the pieces of pale pink organza. Draw round the template with the water-soluble pen or quilter's pencil but do not cut out. Now lay the wadding or batting on the second piece of organza and then place the piece of organza with the wing outline on top. Pin the layers together.

5 Using matching threads, slip stitch the top together on both sides, between the small dot on the sepal trim and the small dot on the bodice. Tie the green organza ribbon round the waist. Remove the original centre of the flower and fasten it to the bow using three strands of yellow embroidery thread and a French knot (see page 14).

2 Using a machine running stitch or hand running stitch, sew all the way around the wing outline. Trim to about 2 mm (½ in) from the stitching. Run a thin line of liquid seam sealant round the wings to prevent them fraying, and leave to dry before securing to the back of the fairy with a few stitches.

OLGA The Russian doll and her daughters

Cuddly Olga is based on Russia's brightly painted nesting wooden dolls, known as Babushka or Matryoshka dolls. Like the most popular of these kinds of dolls Olga is brightly coloured with a cheerful smile and rosy cheeks, and her daughters are minature versions of herself. But unlike her traditional ancestors, Olga is made from snuggly fleece rather than wood.

You will need

MATERIALS
For Olga
- A piece of red fleece measuring approximately 25 x 38 cm (10 x 15 in) (if the fleece has an obvious pile, this should run down the shorter length of the fabric)
- A small piece of cream fleece for the face
- A small piece of yellow fleece for the hair and flower appliqué centres
- A scrap of mid-pink fleece or felt for the cheeks
- A small piece of turquoise fleece for the flower shapes
- Dark grey and red embroidery threads
- A piece of bonding web for the flower appliqués
- 30 g (1 oz) of polyester toy filling
- Matching threads for all your fabrics (except for the cream fleece)

For her daughters
- For each of the smaller dolls you will need slightly smaller quantities of the main fabrics and toy filling. Use the templates on page 102 as a guide.

TOOLS
- Access to a photocopier
- Scissors
- Dressmaking pins
- Water-soluble pen or quilter's pencil
- Sewing machine (optional)
- Sewing needles
- Iron
- A piece of fine cotton such as a handkerchief to protect the appliqué when fixing with the iron

Olga is approximately 21 cm (8¼ in) tall
Her daughters are approximately 17 cm (6¾ in) and 14 cm (5½ in) tall

To make the dolls

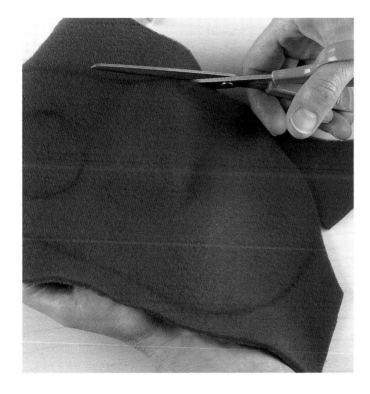

1 Photocopy the front and back body, cheek, hair and face pieces on page 102. Cut out the templates, including the hole for the face on the front body piece. Place the red fleece face down on a hard, flat surface. Place the front body template onto the fleece, making sure that any obvious pile runs down the length of the body shape. Pin the template to the fleece or hold it firmly in place and draw round the template, including the hole for the face, with the water-soluble pen or quilter's pencil, remembering to mark the small dot. Now cut the shape out. Cut out the back body shapes in the same way, making sure that the pile runs down the length of the body and remembering to mark the small dots. Remember that the back body has a right and left side so you will need to cut one piece using the template the right way up and the other using the template face down. Finally, cut out the face from the cream fleece, the hair from the yellow fleece and the two cheeks from the pink fleece or felt.

2 Place the hair right side up on the face, making sure that any obvious pile on the face runs down the length of the face. Pin the hair in place. Machine or hand sew the hair onto the face by stitching very close to the edge along the front curves of the hair.

3 Place the face behind the hole on the front body, making sure that the centre parting of the hair lines up with the dot at the centre of the head. Baste in position. Stitch around the entire edge of the hole for the face using a small machine zig zag stitch and a thread that matches the main body of the doll, or oversew by hand.

4 To make the flowers, photocopy the template on page 102 and trace onto the backing paper of a piece of bonding web, using an ordinary pencil. Next, with the iron on a warm setting, iron the bonding web onto the reverse of the piece of turquoise fleece. Cut the petal shape out carefully. Make two other flower shapes in the same way.

5 Peel off the backing paper of the bonding web and place the flowers in the positions shown on the template. Place a piece of fine cotton, such as a cotton handkerchief, over the flowers to protect them and iron them in position. Secure the appliqués in place by working machine running stitch or hand running stitch round the edge of the petal shapes.

6 To make the flower centres, photocopy the flower centre templates on page 102 and trace onto the bonding web, as described for the petal shapes, and cut them out. Peel off the backing paper, position in the centre of the flowers and iron in place in the same way as the petals. Now machine stitch or hand stitch in position.

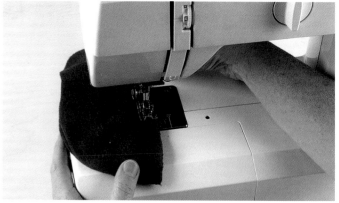

7 Place the two back pieces of the doll right sides together and sew along the back seam, allowing a 5-mm (¼-in) seam allowance and leaving an opening between the two dots, as shown on the template, for stuffing.

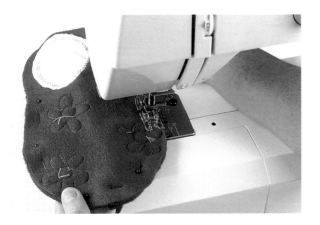

8 Place the back and front pieces of the doll right sides together and pin or baste in position. Now sew around the entire outside of the doll, allowing a 5-mm (¼-in) seam allowance.

9 Turn the doll the right way out through the opening in the back of the doll and stuff fairly firmly, using the blunt end of a pencil to push the stuffing into the head. Close the opening using slip stitch.

10 Mark the position for the eyes, mouth and cheeks with the water-soluble pen or quilter's pencil, using the photograph as a guide. With three strands of dark grey embroidery thread, stitch the eyes by working several 7-mm (¼-in) vertical stitches in and out of the same holes. Add the mouth using back stitch. Draw round the cheek template on the reverse of the pale pink fleece or on the felt and cut out two cheeks. Place the cheeks in position, as shown on the template and oversew them in place. If you are using felt for the cheeks, gently tease round the stitches with the tip of a needle, so that the stitches become almost invisible. (If you use fleece for the cheeks, you do not need to do this.) For added decoration, using a single strand of red embroidery thread, work a star shape over each cheek using large stitches.

Good idea If the flower appliqués seem a bit fiddly, why not make Olga in a floral patterned fleece or embroider a plain fleece with lazy daisy stitches (see page 14-15) worked in knitting wool?

DAISY The baby doll

Rosy-cheeked and bright eyed, Daisy is one of the cutest baby dolls on the planet. In her summery smock with its lace trim she looks the picture of gurgling contentment. She would make a wonderful baby for any little girl to look after and comes complete with her own soft blanket.

You will need

MATERIALS
For the doll
- 2 pieces of pale pink fleece, one measuring approximately 35 x 26 cm (14 x 10¼ in) (if the fleece has an obvious pile, this should run down the longer length of the fabric) and the other measuring approximately 26 x 26 cm (10¼ x 10¼ in)
- A scrap of yellow fleece for the hair
- A scrap of mid-pink fleece or felt for the cheeks
- Dark grey and red embroidery threads
- 35 g (1¼ oz) of polyester toy filling
- Matching threads for all your fabrics

For the clothes and blanket
- A piece of mauve gingham measuring approximately 22 x 50 cm (8¾ x 20 in) for the smock
- 50 cm (20 in) of white lace for the trim
- 2 small buttons for the shoulder straps
- A 20-cm (8-in) length of 7-mm (¼-in) wide mauve ribbon (or a small readymade bow)
- A small piece of purple fleece for the bonnet
- A scrap of white felt for the flower on the bonnet

- A scrap of yellow fleece or felt for the flower centre on the bonnet
- Small pieces of white fleece for the knickers and daisy appliqué on the blanket
- A piece of bright pink fleece measuring 35 x 35 cm (14 x 14 in) for the blanket
- A yellow button for the flower appliqué on the blanket
- A small piece of bonding web for the blanket flower appliqué
- Bright yellow embroidery thread for the blanket
- Matching threads for all your fabrics

TOOLS
- Access to a photocopier
- Scissors
- Dressmaking pins
- Water-soluble pen or quilter's pencil
- Sewing machine (optional)
- Sewing needles
- Iron
- A piece of fine cotton such as a handkerchief to protect the appliqué when fixing with the iron

Daisy is approximately 25 cm (10 in) tall

To make the doll

1 Photocopy the face, back head and body templates for the doll on pages 102-103 and cut them out. With the water-soluble pen or quilter's pencil, mark and cut out one body, one face and two back head pieces from the larger piece of fleece. Remember that the back head has a right and left side so you will need to cut one piece using the template the right way up and the other using the template face down. Remember also to mark the position of the small dots.

2 Pin the two back head pieces right sides together and sew the centre seam, leaving a 5-mm (¼-in) seam allowance and leaving an opening between the small dots.

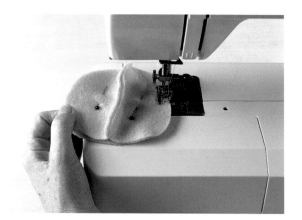

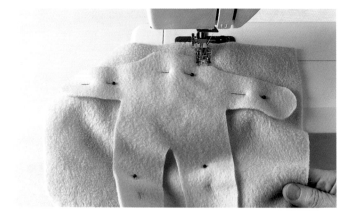

3 Pin or baste the back head to the face so that the right sides of the fabric are together. Seam round the entire face allowing a 5-mm (¼-in) seam allowance. Turn the head the right way out through the back opening and stuff quite firmly. Close the opening using slip stitch.

4 Place the body piece face down on the smaller piece of pink fleece, making sure that any obvious pile on the square of fabric runs down the length of the body shape. Pin or baste in place. Now sew around the outside of the doll, allowing a 5-mm (¼-in) seam allowance, leaving the neck edge open. Trim away the excess fabric on the second piece of fleece to match the doll shape. Make a snip in the seam allowance at the doll's crotch. Turn the doll the right way out and stuff.

5 Tuck the raw edges of the neck inwards and slip stitch the gap closed. Join the head to the body by slip stitching across the neck at the back of the head, so the neck comes about one-third of the way up the back of the head. Turn the doll over and slip stitch the underside of the chin to the front of the neck to secure the head in position.

6 To shape the feet, turn up 4 cm (1½ in) at the end of each leg and hold in place so that the foot is at a right angle to the leg. Now, using the thread double for strength and starting at one of the side seams, work a few large, loose slip stitches across the curve at the front of the ankle. Pull up the thread fairly tightly and secure.

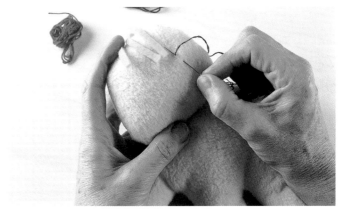

7 To make the hair, cut a few strips of yellow fleece measuring about 8 cm x 5 mm (3¼ x ¼ in). For straight hair like Daisy's, cut the strips across the stretch of the fleece. For curly hair, cut the strips along the stretch of the fleece and pull slightly. Secure the strips across the top seam of the head with a few stitches.

8 Mark the position of the eyes, mouth and cheeks using the water-soluble pen or quilter's pencil. For the eyes, with three strands of dark grey embroidery thread, work three or four 7-mm (¼-in) vertical stitches in and out of the same holes. For the eyelashes, work three separate vertical stitches above each eye. Work the mouth in back stitch using three strands of red embroidery thread. Cut out two cheeks from the pink fleece or felt and oversew them in place.

To make the clothes and accessories

THE SMOCK

1 Photocopy the smock bodice and skirt templates on pages 102-103 and cut them out. Use the templates to cut out four bodice pieces and two skirt pieces. Place two of the bodice pieces right sides together and seam around the sides, shoulders and neck, leaving a 5-mm (¼-in) seam allowance. Do the same with the other two bodice pieces. Clip the corners of the shoulders at the seam allowance, turn rights sides out and press carefully.

2 Gather across the top of the two skirt pieces between the large dots. Turn in 5 mm (¼ in) at each side of the skirt pieces and press. Pull up the gathering so that the top of the skirt is the same width as the base of the bodice. Baste the gathered top of the skirt to the base of one edge of the bodice and seam together, leaving a 5-mm (¼-in) seam al lowance. Remove the gathering stitches. On the inside of the bodice, turn under 5 mm (¼ in) and press. Slip stitch in place. Repeat with the other bodice and skirt piece.

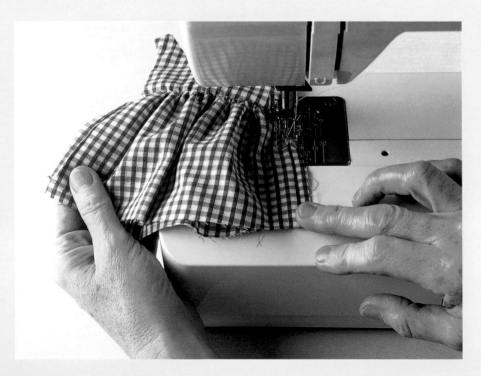

3 Seam the front and back of the smock skirt together at the sides, up to the small dots. Turn the right way out and press. Turn under 1 cm (⅜ in) at the hem edge and press. Turn under another 1 cm (⅜ in) and press again. Stitch close to the folded edge. Overlap the shoulder edgings, stitch in place and add the buttons. Stitch a row of lace round the bottom of the dress and add a bow at the neckline.

THE BONNET

1 Photocopy or trace the templates for the front and back of the bonnet and the flower and flower centre on pages 102-103 and cut them out. Use the template to cut a front and back bonnet from the purple fleece. For the bonnet brim, cut out a strip of purple fleece measuring 2.5 x 28 cm (1 x 11 in), making sure the length of the fabric runs along the stretchy direction of the fleece. Seam the two bonnet pieces together around the sides and top, allowing a 5-mm (¼-in) seam allowance, and trim the seam closely. Turn the edge the right way out.

2 If you are sewing by machine, run a row of zig zag stitch along one of the long sides of the strip. Run a large hand running stitch across the other long edge of the brim. Gather the strip and baste this edge round the base of the bonnet so that the fleecie sides of the strip and bonnet are facing, starting at the centre back. Seam the brim to the bonnet, leaving a 5-mm (¼-in) seam allowance. Trim the seam and turn the bonnet right sides out. Hand stitch the two short edges of the brim together.

3 Using the flower and flower centre template, cut out a flower shape from the white felt and a flower centre from the yellow felt or fleece. Fasten to the bonnet with a couple of stitches through the flower centre, as shown in the photograph.

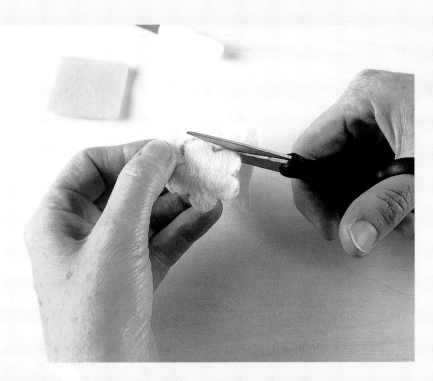

THE BLANKET

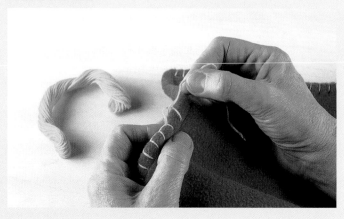

1 Turn under 1 cm (⅜ in) along all the sides of the square of bright pink fleece and baste in position. Work a row of machine or hand running stitch around the blanket edge, close to the raw edge. Now work around the edges of the blanket in blanket stitch (see pages 14–15) using six strands of yellow embroidery thread.

2 To make the daisy appliqué, photocopy the daisy shape on page 103 and trace onto the backing paper of a piece of bonding web, using an ordinary pencil. Next, with the iron on a warm setting, iron the bonding web onto the reverse side of the small piece of white fleece then cut the shape out. Peel off the backing paper of the bonding web and place the daisy in the position shown on the template. Cover with a piece of fine cotton such as a cotton handkerchief and iron in position. Use a machine running stitch or hand stitch round the daisy to secure it and add the yellow button for the centre.

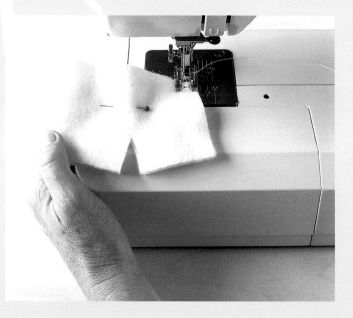

THE KNICKERS

Photocopy the template for the knickers on page 103 and cut it out. Use the template to cut out two knicker shapes from the white fleece. Seam at the sides and crotch. Trim the seams and turn the right way out.

Good idea For a baby boy, omit the frill and flower on the bonnet to make a simple pull-on hat and use the pattern for the knickers to create some matching shorts. Leave the blanket plain or use the heart template for Abbie & Alfie on page 98 to add a heart appliqué.

MAGNUS The little monster

Although this little fellow's eyes are wonky and his skin a bright shade of green, his toothy grin is guaranteed to melt even the hardest of hearts. He is made from just two pieces of fabric seamed together and is one of the very easiest projects in the book. So if you're new to sewing, he's an ideal place to start and would make the perfect gift for little monsters everywhere.

You will need

MATERIALS

- 2 pieces of lime green fleece, each measuring 32 x 20 cm (12½ x 8 in) (if the fleece has an obvious pile, this should run down the longer length of the fabric)
- Scraps of black, white and mid-blue felt for the eyes
- A 20-cm (8-in) strip of wide ric rac braid in deep pink for the antennae
- A selection of brightly coloured small buttons in different shapes and sizes
- Red and white embroidery threads
- 25 g (1 oz) of polyester toy filling
- Matching threads for all your fabrics
- Liquid seam sealant (to prevent ric rac braid from fraying)

TOOLS

- Access to a photocopier
- Scissors
- Dressmaking pins
- Water-soluble pen or quilter's pencil
- Sewing machine (optional)
- Sewing needles

Magnus is approximately 30 cm (12 in) tall

To make the doll

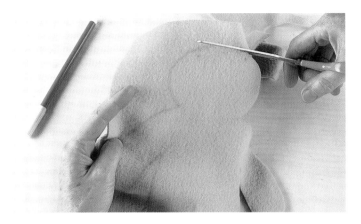

1 Photocopy the body template and the eye templates on page 104 and cut them out. Place the body template onto one piece of green fleece, making sure that any obvious pile runs down the length of the body shape. Draw round the template with the water-soluble pen or quilter's pencil, remembering to mark the small dots. Now cut the shape out. Remember, you only need to cut out one body shape at this stage.

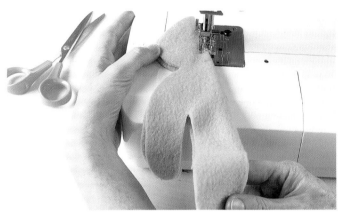

2 Fold the body piece in half lengthways so that the fleecie side of the fabric is on the inside. Sew the body dart – from the centre of the face into the neck, then from the neck outwards to the tummy – using a small running stitch or medium length machine stitch.

3 Cut the ric rac braid into three pieces and treat the ends with liquid seam sealant to stop them fraying. Baste the ric rac strips to the right side of the fabric, at the top of the head in the position indicated on the pattern. The base of the pieces of ric rac should slightly overlap the raw edge of the head and point inwards towards the face.

4 Lay the doll shape face down on the second piece of fleece, making sure the pile runs down the length of the fabric, and pin or baste in place. Sew around the outside of the doll, leaving a 5-mm (¼-in) seam allowance and leaving an opening for stuffing, as shown on the template. Trim away the excess fabric. Make a snip in the seam allowance at the doll's crotch to help prevent any puckering. Turn the doll the right way out through the opening and stuff. Slip stitch the opening closed.

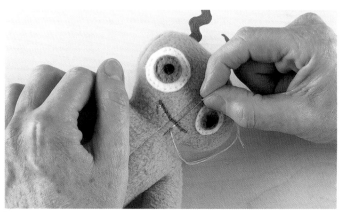

5 Cut the templates for the eyes out – the outer circles in white, the middle circles in blue and the inner circles in black felt. Position the eyes and sew round each circle in matching thread, using tiny running stitches.

6 Mark the position for the mouth using the water-soluble pen or quilter's pencil using the photograph as a guide. With three strands of red embroidery thread, work a row of chain stitch (see pages 13–14). Work the teeth by working four small single chain stitches along the bottom of the mouth.

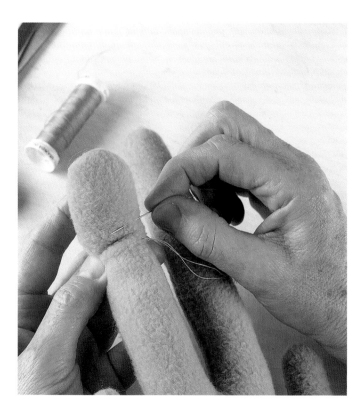

7 To shape the feet, turn up 6 cm (2½ in) at the end of each leg and hold in place so that the foot is at a right angle to the leg. Now, using the thread double for strength and starting at one of the side seams, work a few large, loose slip stitches across the curve at the front of the ankle. Pull up the thread fairly tightly and secure. For his claws, use three strands of red embroidery thread. Secure the thread invisibly in the side seam and take the needle out through the top of the foot ready to sew the first claw. Now take the thread over the end of the foot, through the back and out through the front, ready to work the next claw. Work two more claws in the same way and secure the thread in the side seam. Finish the monster doll by decorating with the buttons.

RUBY & ZAK The tiny twosome

These charming pocket-sized companions are really quick and simple to make and are perfect to take out on trips as they take up so little space. As they're so tiny, you'll need hardly any fabric to make them and they are an ideal way of using up your scraps.

You will need

MATERIALS

For the dolls
- 2 pieces of cream or mid-brown fleece, each measuring 18 x 20 cm (7 x 8 in) (if the fleece has an obvious pile, this should run down the longer length of the fabric)
- A small piece of orange or black fleece for the hair (depending on which doll you are making)
- A scrap of pale pink felt for Ruby's cheeks or mid-pink felt for Zak's cheeks
- Black and red embroidery threads
- 15 g (½ oz) of polyester toy filling
- Matching threads for all your fabrics
- Fabric glue

For the clothes and hair accessories

For Ruby
- A small piece of purple fleece for the dress
- Matching thread
- A small green button
- 20 cm (8 in) of 7-mm (¼-in) wide lime green ribbon

For Zak
- A small piece of yellow fleece for the top
- A small piece of turquoise fleece for the shorts
- A scrap of red fleece for the star appliqué
- A small piece of bonding web for the appliqué
- Matching threads for all your fabrics

TOOLS
- Access to a photocopier
- Pencil (for Zak only)
- Scissors
- Dressmaking pins
- Water-soluble pen or quilter's pencil
- Sewing machine (optional)
- Hole punch
- Iron (for Zak only)
- A piece of fine cotton such as a handkerchief to protect the appliqué when fixing with the iron (for Zak only)

Ruby & Zak are approximately 16 cm (6¼ in) tall

To make the dolls

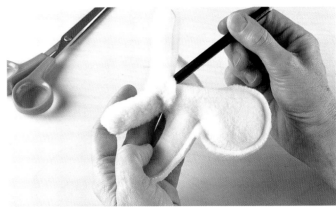

1 Photocopy the doll and hair templates on pages 104–105 and cut them out. Place the body template onto the fleece for the body, making sure that any obvious pile runs down the length of the shape. Draw round the template with the water-soluble pen or quilter's pencil, remembering to mark the small dots, and cut the shape out. You only need to cut out one body shape at this stage.

2 Now lay the doll shape face down on the second piece of fleece and pin or baste in place. Sew around the outside of the doll, allowing a 5-mm (¼-in) seam allowance and leaving an opening for stuffing, as shown on the template. Trim away the excess fabric to match the doll shape, taking care not to cut through the stitching. Snip the seam allowance at the doll's crotch. Turn the doll the right way out and stuff. Close the opening using slip stitch.

3 Cut out the front and back pieces for the hair using the templates. For Zak's hair, sew the small dart at the back as indicated on the template. Place the hair pieces right sides together and seam round the top, allowing a 5-mm (¼-in) seam allowance. Trim the seam closely and turn the hair the right way out. For Zak, oversew in place round the entire edge of the hair. For Ruby, work a few small running stitches across the top of the head.

4 Mark the position of the eyes and mouth using the water-soluble pen or quilter's pencil. For the eyes, with three strands of black embroidery thread, work three or four 5-mm (¼-in) vertical stitches in and out of the same holes. Using three strands of red embroidery thread, work the mouth using back stitch. Using the hole punch, press out two circles of pink felt. Glue each cheek in position. Work a cross-shaped stitch over each cheek to secure.

To make the clothes

FOR RUBY

1 Photocopy the dress template on page 104 and cut it out. Use the template to cut out two dress pieces from the purple fleece, making sure that any obvious pile runs down the length of the dress. Place the two dress pieces right sides together and seam together at the shoulders, allowing a 5-mm (¼-in) seam allowance. Trim the seam allowance. If you are sewing by machine, work a small zig zag stitch round the entire neck edge of the dress. This helps give a professional finish but is not essential.

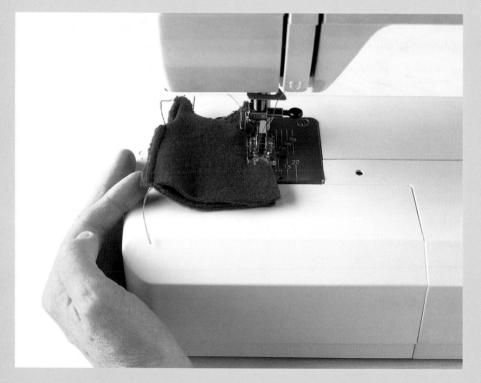

2 Sew the side seams of the dress, again allowing a 5-mm (¼-in) seam allowance. Trim the side seams. If you are sewing by machine, work a small zig zag stitch round the bottom of the dress. Again, this helps give a professional finish but is not essential. Sew the button to the front of the dress and tie the green ribbon into a small bow and stitch it to Ruby's hair, as shown in the photograph.

FOR ZAK

1 Photocopy the templates for the shorts and jumper on page 105 and cut them out. Use the templates to cut out two jumper pieces from the yellow fleece and two shorts pieces from the turquoise fleece, making sure any obvious pile runs down the length of the pieces. To make the star appliqué, trace the star shape on page 105 onto the backing paper of a piece of bonding web, using an ordinary pencil. Next, with the iron on a warm setting, iron the bonding web onto the reverse side of the scrap of red fleece then cut the star out. Peel off the backing paper of the bonding web and place the star in the position shown on the template. Cover the appliqué with a piece of fine cotton, such as a cotton handkerchief, and iron in position. Secure the star by machine stitching round the outer edge or oversewing by hand.

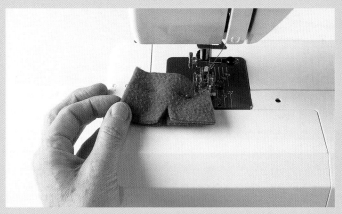

2 Place the two jumper pieces right sides together. Seam along the top of the sleeves and then the lower edge of the sleeves and jumper sides, allowing a 5-mm (¼-in) seam allowance. Trim the seams then turn the jumper the right way out. If you are sewing by machine, work a small zig zag stitch round the bottom edge of the jumper. This helps give a professional finish but is not essential.

3 For the shorts, place the two pieces right sides together. Seam along the sides of the shorts and the inner leg edges. Trim the seams and turn the shorts the right way out.

TILLY The mermaid

Beautiful, flame-haired Tilly would enchant even the hardest-hearted crews on the open waves. Her turquoise tail is adorned with shell-like sequins and her hair enhanced with a rippled fancy yarn to give it a sea-worn look. Her bikini top, made from a piece of organza ribbon, completes her shimmery seaside look.

You will need

MATERIALS
For the doll

- 2 pieces of cream fleece, each measuring 13 x 23 cm (5¼ x 9 in) (if the fleece has an obvious pile, this should run down the shorter length of the fabric)
- 2 pieces of turquoise fleece, each measuring 18 x 10 cm (7 x 4 in) (if the fleece has an obvious pile, this should run down the longer length of the fabric)
- A piece of orange fleece for the hair, measuring 6 x 30 cm (2½ x 12 in) (the length of the fabric should run along the most stretchy part of the fleece)
- Approximately 1.8 m (6 ft) of fancy orange/yellow yarn
- A scrap of mid-pink fleece or felt for the cheeks
- Approximately 25 standard sequins in a mixture of pale pink and green
- Dark grey and lime green embroidery threads
- 20 g (¾ oz) of polyester toy filling
- Matching thread for your fabrics

For the bikini top
- A 12-cm (4¾-in) length of 5-cm (2-in) wide olive green organza ribbon
- Matching thread
- A short length of lime green embroidery thread
- A small mother of pearl button
- Liquid seam sealant (to prevent the ribbon fraying)

TOOLS
- Access to a photocopier
- Scissors
- Dressmaking pins
- Water-soluble pen or quilter's pencil
- Sewing machine (optional)
- Sewing needles

Tilly is approximately 26 cm (10¼ in) tall

To make the doll

1 Photocopy or trace the mermaid body, tail and cheek templates on page 105 and cut them out. Place one piece of the cream fleece face down on a hard, flat surface. Place the body template onto the fleece, making sure that any obvious pile runs down the length of the body shape. Pin the template to the fleece or hold it firmly in place and draw round the template with the water-soluble pen or quilter's pencil, remembering to mark the small dots. Now cut the shape out. Remember, you only need to cut out one body shape at this stage.

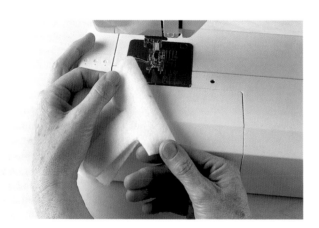

2 Fold the body piece in half lengthways so that the fleecie side of the fabric is on the inside. Sew the body dart – from the centre of the face into the neck, then from the neck outwards to the tummy – using a small running stitch or medium length machine stitch.

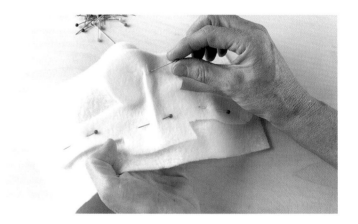

3 Now lay the doll front face down on the second piece of fleece, making sure that any obvious pile runs down the length of the fabric, and pin or baste in place. Sew around the outside of the doll, allowing a 5-mm (¼-in) seam allowance, leaving the bottom of the body open. Trim away the excess fabric on the second piece of fleece to match the doll shape, taking care not to cut through the stitching. Turn the doll the right way out and stuff fairly gently.

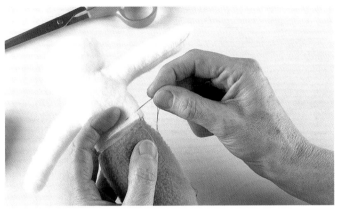

4 To make the tail, use the template to cut out one tail from one of the pieces of turquoise fleece, making sure that any obvious pile runs down the length of the tail. Lay the tail shape right side down on the second piece of fleece and pin or baste in position. Sew round the tail, leaving a 5-mm (¼-in) seam allowance and leaving it open at the top (waist) end. Trim away the excess fabric. Turn the tail the right way out and stuff.

5 Join the body to the tail by slip stitching round the waist of the doll, using your thread double for extra strength. Decorate the tail with sequins as shown in the photograph and, using three strands of lime green embroidery thread, work three lines of back stitch on each side of the tail fin.

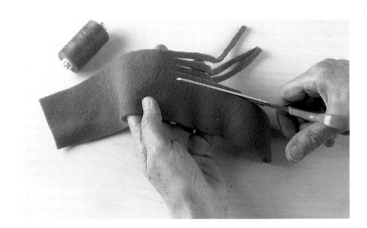

6 To make the hair, cut into the fleece every 5 mm (¼ in) across the two shorter edges, stopping just short of the centre parting. Cut the fancy yarn into six 30-cm (12-in) lengths. Position the fleece hair across the head so that the hair begins about 1.5 cm (¾ in) below the seam at the top of the head, on the doll's forehead. Secure the hair in place by backstitching along the centre parting, using your thread double for extra strength and sewing in the strands of fancy yarn at regular intervals.

7 Mark the position of the features using the water-soluble pen or quilter's pencil, using the photograph as a guide. For the eyes, with three strands of dark grey embroidery thread, work three or four 7-mm (¼-in) vertical stitches in and out of the same holes. Work the mouth in back stitch. Draw round the cheek template on the reverse of the pale pink fleece or on the felt and cut out two cheeks. Place the cheeks in position, as shown on the template and oversew them in place.

To make the bikini top

1 Fold the length of ribbon in half widthways and seam down the shorter edges, leaving a 5-mm (¼-in) seam allowance (you may find this easier to do by hand). Trim the seam and run a length of seam sealant along the raw edges to prevent any fraying.

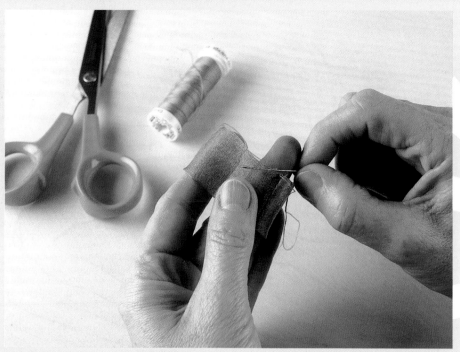

2 Now fold the hoop of ribbon in half, so the seam is on the inside. Slip stitch the long sides of the ribbon together. Now put the top on the doll. Cut a length of lime green embroidery thread and tie it round the middle of the bikini top. Fasten the bikini strap at the back of the dolls neck. Complete the top by sewing on the button, as shown in the photograph.

Good idea Instead of a bikini top, try sewing two small shell buttons on Tilly to create an eye-catching bra top.

JOHNNIE the friendly alien

Johnnie is probably the least scary alien you'll ever come across. Based on the popular 'gonks'

of 1970s childhoods, he has been brought right up to date but maintains a slightly retro air.

With his lopsided smile and friendly expression, he would make a great companion for small

boys everywhere.

You will need

MATERIALS
- A piece of orange fleece, measuring 28 x 25 cm (11 x 10 in) (if the fleece has an obvious pile, this should run down the shorter length of the fabric)
- A piece of turquoise fleece, measuring 19 x 24 cm (7½ x 9½ in) (if the fleece has an obvious pile, this should run down the shorter length of the fabric)
- A small piece of cream fleece for the face
- A small piece of yellow fleece for the 'belt'
- A small piece of bonding web for fixing the face
- A 20-cm (8-in) length of green ric rac braid to decorate the belt
- A 20-cm (8-in) length of decorative blue ribbon to decorate the belt
- Purple embroidery thread
- 20 g (¾ oz) of polyester toy filling
- Matching thread for all your fabrics and for the ric rac braid and decorative ribbon
- 2 odd sized coloured buttons for the eyes

TOOLS
- Access to a photocopier
- Pencil
- Scissors
- Dressmaking pins
- Water-soluble pen or quilter's pencil
- Sewing machine (optional)
- Sewing needles
- Iron
- A piece of fine cotton such as a handkerchief to protect the face when fixing with the iron

Johnnie is approximately 30 cm (12 in) tall

To make the doll

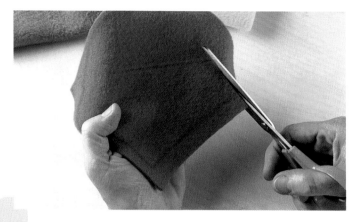

1 Photocopy the templates for the alien doll's body, nose, arms, belt and legs on page 106 and cut them out. Cut out two body pieces and four arm pieces from the orange fleece, two belt pieces from the yellow fleece and two leg pieces from the turquoise fleece.

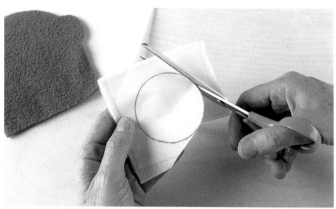

2 To make the face, photocopy the face shape on page 106 and trace onto the backing paper of a piece of bonding web, using an ordinary pencil. Next, with the iron on a warm setting, iron the bonding web onto the reverse of the piece of cream fleece. Now cut the shape out.

3 Peel off the backing paper of the bonding web and place the face on one of the body pieces in the position shown on the template, making sure that any obvious pile runs down the length of the face. Place a piece of fine cotton, such as a cotton handkerchief, over the face and iron in position. Secure the face by working a small machine zig zag stitch round the outside edge or oversew by hand.

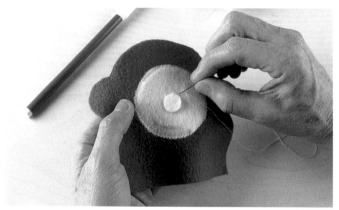

4 Draw round the nose template on the back of a scrap of cream fleece used for the face and cut it out. Position the nose just below the centre point of the face and oversew in place by hand. Using the photograph as a guide, draw the mouth using the water-soluble pen or quilter's pencil. Embroider the mouth in chain stitch (see pages 13–14), using three strands of purple embroidery thread.

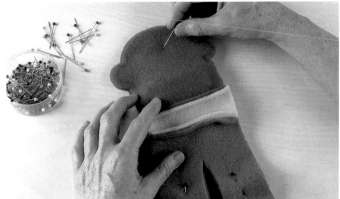

5 Using thread to match the belt, seam the body, belt and leg pieces together so that you have two complete doll pieces. Place two arm pieces right sides together and seam together, leaving them open at the end and allowing a 5-mm (¼-in) seam allowance. Turn the right way out but do not stuff. Do the same with the other two arm pieces. Baste the arms to the body in the position indicated on the template on the right side of one of the body pieces.

6 Place the two doll pieces right sides together and pin or baste in position. Seam round the doll using matching threads. Remember to take particular care around the ears. Leave a 5-mm (¼-in) seam allowance and leave an opening for stuffing between the two small dots. Turn the doll the right way out and stuff fairly lightly. Close the opening using slip stitch.

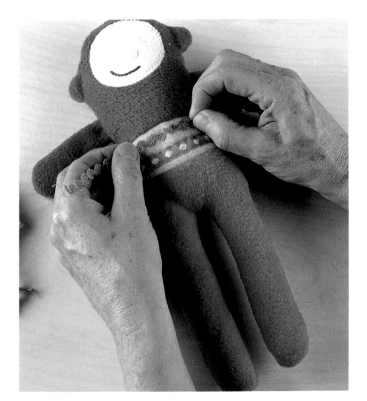

7 Hand stitch the ric rac braid round the belt using a small running stitch. Hand stitch the ribbon in place by slip stitching along both long edges. Finish the alien doll by sewing on the button eyes, using the photograph as a guide.

Good idea You can really let your imagination go wild when making these little fellows. Gather together your stash of fleece and braids and try out some exciting new colour combinations.

JASMINE The leggy babe

Beautiful Jasmine will feel right at home in the bedroom of any fashion-conscious girl. With her short skirt and matching bag and boots, it's obvious she's a slave to fashion and just wants to have fun. Choose your own colours and have fun creating your own leggy teen who promises not to have a single tantrum.

You will need

MATERIALS

For the doll

- A piece of mid-brown fleece, measuring 48 x 52 cm (19 x 20½ in) (if the fabric has an obvious pile, this should run down the longer length of the fabric)
- A piece of black fleece for the hair, measuring 23 x 8 cm (9 x 3¼ in) (this should be cut so that the stretch of the fabric lies along the longer length of the fabric)
- A piece of red fleece for the boots, measuring 24 x 16 cm (9½ x 6¼ in) (if the fabric has an obvious pile, this should run down the shorter length of the fabric)
- Scraps of white and black felt for the eyes
- A scrap of bright pink felt for the lips
- Black embroidery thread
- 80 g (3 oz) of polyester toy filling
- Matching threads for all your fabrics, including the felt

For the clothes and bag

- A piece of floral cotton or cotton mix fabric for the skirt measuring 17 x 37 cm (6¾ x 14½ in) (if the fabric has an obvious direction the pattern should run up the shorter length of the fabric)
- A 25-cm (10-in) length of elastic cord for the waist of the skirt
- A piece of yellow fleece for the vest top, measuring 28 x 15 cm (11 x 6 in) (if the fleece has an obvious pile, this should run down the shorter length of the fabric)
- A piece of turquoise fleece for the cropped cardigan, measuring 16 x 32 cm (6¼ x 12½ in) (if the fleece has an obvious pile, this should run down the shorter length of the fabric)
- A short length of turquoise embroidery thread for the button hole fastening
- A medium-sized green button

- A piece of red fleece for the bag, measuring 13 x 22 cm (5¼ x 8¾ in) (if the fleece has an obvious pile, this should run down the longer length of the fabric) plus a strip of red fleece measuring 1.5 x 36 cm (¾ x 14 in) (ideally this should be cut so that the stretch of the fabric lies along the shorter width of the fabric)
- A medium-sized yellow heart shaped button to decorate the bag
- Matching threads for all your fabrics

TOOLS

- Access to a photocopier
- Scissors
- Dressmaking pins
- Water-soluble pen or quilter's pencil
- Sewing machine (optional)
- Sewing needles
- Iron
- Small safety pin for threading the elastic cord

Jasmine is approximately 69 cm (27 in) tall

To make the doll

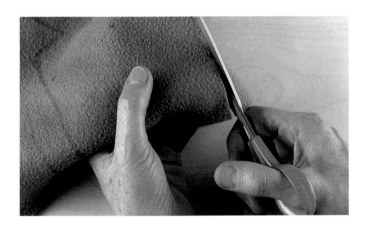

1 Photocopy the head and body, arm, leg, boot, eye and lip templates on pages 106–107 and cut them out. Pin the templates onto the fleece and trace round them using the water-soluble pen or quilter's pencil. Cut out two head and body pieces, four arm and four leg pieces from the mid-brown fleece. From the red fleece, cut out four boot pieces. Make sure that any obvious pile runs down the length of the body pieces and mark the position of the small dots.

2 Fold one of the head and body pieces in half lengthwise, right sides together, and sew the body dart – from the centre of the face into the neck, then from the neck outwards to the tummy – using a small running stitch. Place the two head and body pieces right sides together. Pin or baste in position and seam round the outside, leaving a 5-mm (¼-in) seam allowance. Leave open between the two sets of small dots for inserting the arms and at the bottom. Turn the body piece the right way out.

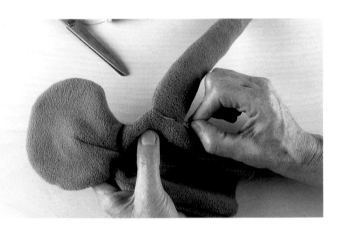

3 Place two of the arm pieces right sides together and pin or baste in position. Seam round the outside, leaving a 5-mm (¼-in) seam allowance. Leave the end open for turning and stuffing. Do the same with the other two arm pieces. Turn the arms the right way out and stuff fairly lightly. Insert the arms through the holes in the sides of the body, tucking the raw edges inwards. Slip stitch in place using your thread double for extra strength. Now stuff the head and body piece.

4 Seam the top (flat end) of the red boot pieces to the bottom of the leg pieces, allowing a 5-mm (¼-in) seam allowance. Now place two of the leg pieces right sides together. Pin or baste in position then seam round the outside in matching threads, again leaving a 5-mm (¼-in) seam allowance and leaving the top open for turning and stuffing. Do the same with the other two leg pieces. Turn the legs the right way out and stuff the boots quite firmly and the legs fairly lightly.

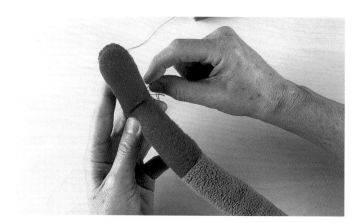

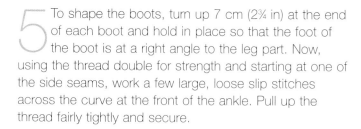

5 To shape the boots, turn up 7 cm (2¾ in) at the end of each boot and hold in place so that the foot of the boot is at a right angle to the leg part. Now, using the thread double for strength and starting at one of the side seams, work a few large, loose slip stitches across the curve at the front of the ankle. Pull up the thread fairly tightly and secure.

6 Turn under 5 mm (¼ in) along the lower edge of the body and baste. Insert the top of the legs into the body so that the edges of the legs line up with the sides of the body. Slip stitch in place using your thread double for extra strength and slip stitch across the crotch.

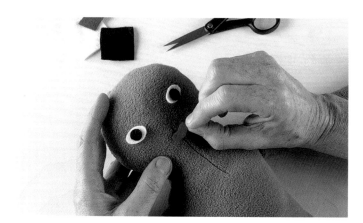

7 Cut out two outer eyes from white felt, two inner eyes from black felt and the lips from bright pink felt. Using the photograph as a guide, position the eyes and lips and oversew them in place. When you have finished, gently tease round the stitches with the tip of a needle, so that the stitches become almost invisible. For the eyelashes, work three large stitches at the outer corner of each eye using three strands of black embroidery thread.

8 For the hair, cut the black fleece into 3-mm (⅛-in) strips along its length. Starting on the forehead, 2 cm (¾ in) down from the centre seam of the head, back stitch the hair in place, ending 3 or 4 cm (1¼ or 1½ in) above the back of the neck. You may find it helpful to draw a sewing line using the water-soluble pen or quilter's pencil before you start. Trim the hair at the back slightly to make it neater. To give the hair a slight curl, pull each strand separately and allow it to spring back.

To make the vest top

1 Photocopy the vest top template on page 107 and cut it out. Cut out two vest pieces from the yellow fleece making sure that any obvious pile runs down the length of the top. Place the two vest top pieces right sides together and sew the shoulder seams, allowing a 5-mm (¼-in) seam allowance. Trim the seams closely. If you are using a sewing machine, machine around the neck opening using a small zig zag stitch. This gives a professional finish, but is not essential.

2 Sew the side seams of the vest top, again allowing a 5-mm (¼-in) seam allowance and trim. If you are using a sewing machine, machine around the bottom of the vest top using a small zig zag stitch, stretching the fabric slightly as you sew.

To make the cardigan

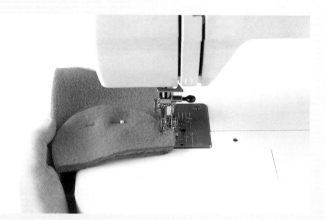

1 Photocopy the cardigan front, back and sleeve templates on pages 106–107 and cut them out. Use the templates to cut out one cardigan back, two fronts (one using the template the right way up and one using the template face down) and two sleeves from the turquoise fleece, remembering to mark the small dots. Make sure that any obvious pile runs down the length of the pieces. Sew the shoulder seams leaving a 5-mm, (¼-in) seam allowance and trim close to the seams.

2 With the fabric pieces right sides together, position the sleeves face down on the right side of the cardigan, between the small dots across the shoulder, making sure that the pile runs down the length of the sleeve. Stitch together leaving a 5-mm (¼-in) seam allowance. Now stitch the side and arm seams, again leaving a 5-mm (¼-in) seam allowance. If you are using a sewing machine, machine around the entire cardigan using a small zig zag stitch. This isn't essential but helps give the cardigan a professional finish.

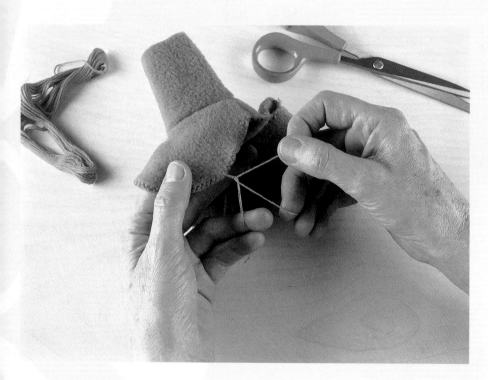

3 Complete the cardigan by sewing the button in place. Make the button hole with a piece of turquoise embroidery thread. Thread the piece through the cardigan front in the position marked by the small dot. Divide the twelve strands into three groups of four. Make a plait about 2 cm (¾ in) long. Thread the twelve strands back through the position marked by the second dot, from front to back. Divide the threads into two groups and knot together to secure.

To make the skirt

1 Fold the skirt fabric in half widthways so that the pattern is on the inside, and stitch the back seam, leaving a 5-mm (¼-in) seam allowance. Press seam open. For the hem, Turn down 1 cm (⅜ in) at the bottom edge and press in place. Turn down another 1 cm (⅜ in) and press again. Stitch close to the folded edge using a machine running stitch or hand hemming stitch.

2 For the casing, prepare the fabric and stitch as for the hem, but leave a 1-cm (⅜-in) opening at the back seam for threading the elastic cord. Using the small safety pin, thread the elastic through the casing. Knot the ends together tightly and trim.

To make the bag

1 Photocopy or trace the bag front and back templates on page 107 and cut them out. Use the templates to cut out one back and one front bag piece from the red fleece, making sure that any obvious pile runs down the length of both pieces. Pin the bag front and back right sides together and seam round the sides and bottom of the bag, leaving the front flap free. Turn the bag the right way out.

2 To finish, overlap the ends of the strip of red fleece about 1 cm (⅜ in) on either side of the bag and oversew in position. Sew the yellow heart button to the flap, as shown in the main photograph.

PEDRO The pirate

In his smart red and black striped trousers, Pedro is ready for a life of adventure on the high seas. He cuts a dashing figure with his hat and cutlass but underneath it all, he's just a big softie. Pedro is made from two pieces of fabric and his fancy-looking clothes are also deceptively simple to create.

You will need

MATERIALS
For the doll
- 2 pieces of mid-brown fleece, each measuring 28 x 37 cm (11 x 14½ in) (if the fleece has an obvious pile, this should run down the longer length of the fabric)
- Black and dark red embroidery threads
- A scrap of black fleece for the hair
- 20 g (¾ oz) of polyester toy filling
- Matching thread for your fabrics

For the clothes and cutlass
- A piece of white fleece for the shirt, measuring 26 x 22 cm (10¼ x 8¾ in) (the pile of the fabric should run down the longer length of the fleece)
- A piece of red fleece for the waistcoat, measuring 12 x 24 cm (4¾ x 9½ in)
- A piece of red and black striped cotton or polycotton fabric for the trousers, measuring 19 x 32 cm (7½ x 12½ in) (the stripe should run down the shorter length of the fabric)

Pedro is approximately 28 cm (11 in) tall

- Small pieces of black and white felt for the hat
- Black and white embroidery threads
- A scrap of red polka dot fabric for the scarf
- A small piece of metallic silver fabric for the cutlass
- A 30-cm (12-in) length of 1-cm (⅜-in) wide black ribbon for the belt
- A 20-cm (8-in) length of elastic cord
- Matching threads for all your fabrics
- Liquid seam sealant
- Fabric glue (optional)

TOOLS
- Access to a photocopier
- Scissors
- Dressmaking pins
- Water-soluble pen or quilter's pencil
- Sewing machine (optional)
- Sewing needles
- Iron
- Small safety pin for threading the elastic cord

To make the doll

1 Photocopy the body and hair templates on page 108 and cut them out. Place the body template onto the mid-brown fleece, making sure that any obvious pile runs down the length of the body shape. Draw round the template with the water-soluble pen or quilter's pencil, remembering to mark the small dots. Now cut the shape out. Remember, you only need to cut out one body shape at this stage.

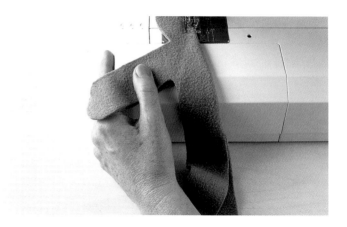

2 Fold the body piece in half lengthways so that the fleecie side of the fabric is on the inside. Sew the body dart – from the centre of the face into the neck, then from the neck outwards to the tummy – using a small running stitch or medium length machine stitch.

3 Now place your second piece of mid-brown fleece face up on a hard surface, making sure any obvious pile runs down the length of the fabric. Lay the doll shape face down on the second piece of fleece and pin or baste in place. Now sew around the outside of the doll, allowing a 5-mm (¼-in) seam allowance and leaving an opening for stuffing, as shown on the template. Trim away the excess fabric on the second piece of fleece to match the doll shape. Make a snip in the seam allowance at the doll's crotch. This will help prevent any puckering round the crotch on the finished toy. Turn the doll the right way out through the opening and stuff. Stuff the head quite firmly and the body more lightly. Close the opening using slip stitch.

4 To shape the feet, turn up 4 cm (1½ in) at the end of each foot and hold in place so that the foot is at a right angle to the leg. Now, using the thread double for strength and starting at one of the side seams, work a few large, loose slip stitches across the curve at the front of the ankle. Pull up the thread fairly tightly and secure.

5 Use the hair template to cut out the hair shape, making sure that the length of the hair shape runs along the stretch of the fleece. Stretch the strip of black fleece along the top seam of the head and oversew in place.

6 Mark the position of the eyes and mouth using the water-soluble pen or quilter's pencil, using the photograph as a guide. For the eyes, with three strands of black embroidery thread, work three or four 7-mm (¼-in) vertical stitches in and out of the same holes. With three strands of dark red embroidery thread, work the mouth in back stitch.

To make the shirt

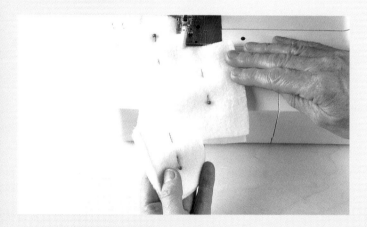

1 Use the shirt template on page 108 to cut two shirt shapes from the white fleece. With the right sides of the shirt together, seam the shirt along the top of the arms and the under arm and side seams, allowing a 5-mm (¼-in) seam allowance.

2 Trim the seams and cut the shirt down the centre on one side. Turn the shirt the right way out. If you are using a sewing machine, run a line of small zig zag stitching round the entire raw edges of the shirt. This isn't essential but it gives the garment a professional finish.

To make the waistcoat

1 Photocopy the waistcoat templates on page 109 and cut them out. Use the templates to cut out one back and two front waistcoat pieces from the red fleece. Because the waistcoat has a right and left side, you will need to cut one front piece using the template the right way up and one using it face down. With the waistcoat pieces right sides together, seam the waistcoat at the shoulders and sides, leaving a 5-mm (¼-in) seam allowance. Trim the seams and turn the waistcoat the right way out.

To make the trousers

1 Photocopy the trousers template on page 108 and cut it out. Cut out two pieces of striped cotton, making sure the stripes run down the length of the trousers. Lay the two pieces of fabric right sides together and sew the crotch seams, allowing a 5-mm (¼-in) seam allowance. Press the seams open with the iron.

2 Keeping the right sides of the fabric facing, match the front and back crotch seams and stitch the inside leg seams, again allowing a 5-mm (¼-in) seam allowance. Press the seams open.

3 To make the waistband, turn down 1 cm (⅜ in) at the top raw edge and press in place. Turn down another 1 cm (⅜ in) and press again. Stitch as close as possible to the folded edge, leaving a 1-cm (¼-in) opening at the back of the trousers for threading the elastic cord. Using the small safety pin, thread the elastic cord through the waistband casing. Pull the elastic up, knot the ends together tightly and trim.

Good idea If you don't want to make the pirate hat, wrap a triangle of spotted red fabric round Pedro's head, a bit like a head scarf, and knot it at the back. If necessary, secure with a few stitches. You could also make him an eye patch from a small scrap of felt and a piece of black elastic cord.

To make the hat and cravat

1 Use the hat and skull motif templates to cut out two hat shapes from the black felt and one skull shape from the white felt. Stick or oversew the motif in place. Using six strands of white embroidery thread, work a large cross underneath the skull motif. With three strands of black embroidery thread, work two French knots (see page 14) on the skull motif for eyes and a small horizontal stitch for the mouth.

2 Place the two pieces of the hat together and work a small running stitch round the sides and top. For the cravat, cut out a scrap of red polka dot fabric about 17 x 2 cm (6¾ x ¾ in) and tie in a single knot around Pedro's neck.

To make the cutlass and belt

1 Photocopy the cutlass motif on page 108 and cut it out. Place the cutlass template on a small piece of the silver metallic fabric. Draw round the template with the water-soluble pen or quilter's pencil but do not cut out. Now lay the wadding or batting on another small piece of the metallic fabric and then place the piece of fabric with the cutlass outline on top. Pin the layers together.

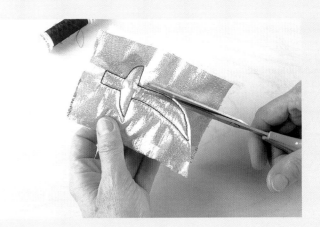

2 Using a machine running stitch or hand running stitch and black thread, sew all the way around the cutlass outline. Trim to about 2 mm (1/12 in) from the stitching. Run a thin line of liquid seam sealant round the cutlass to prevent it fraying and leave to dry. Tie the length of black ribbon around Pedro's waist and tuck the cutlass into it.

MIMI & LOUIS *The ultra-cool doll and her puppy*

Mimi is based on the 'amigurumu' knitted dolls that are so popular in Japan. With her huge eyes and trendy outfit – not to mention her adorable puppy - she's sure to catch any boy's eye. Mimi is a must have for modern girls everywhere.

You will need

MATERIALS
For the doll
- A piece of cream fleece, measuring 20 x 30 cm (8 x 12 in) (if the fabric has an obvious pile, this should run down the shorter length of the fabric)
- A piece of striped fleece, measuring 11 x 21 cm (4½ x 8¼ in) for the dress, which is sewn as part of the doll. The stripe should run across the longer length of the fleece
- A piece of dark grey fleece measuring 6 x 15 cm (2½ x 6 in) for the hair
- Scraps of pale blue and black felt for the eyes
- Red embroidery thread
- 15–20 g (½–¾ oz) polyester toy filling
- Matching threads for all your fabrics, including the felt

For the hat and scarf
- A small piece of bright pink fleece for the hat
- A piece of lime green fleece measuring 29 x 1 cm (11½ x ⅜ in) for the scarf
- A scrap of yellow felt for the flower

Mimi is approximately 21 cm (8¼ in) tall

- A red button for the flower centre
- Matching thread for your main fabric

For Louis the puppy
- 2 pieces of pale grey fleece each measuring 11 x 8 cm (4½ x 3¼ in)
- Matching thread
- Black embroidery thread
- A small amount of polyester toy filling
- A 30-cm (12-in) length of 5-mm (¼-in) wide red ribbon for the lead

TOOLS
- Access to a photocopier
- Scissors
- Dressmaking pins
- Water-soluble pen or quilter's pencil
- Sewing machine (optional)
- Sewing needles

To make the doll

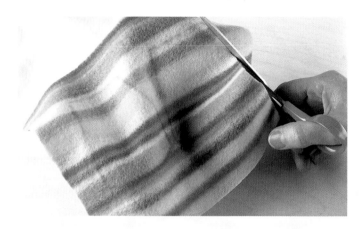

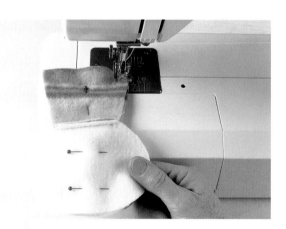

1 Photocopy the head, dress, limb and eye templates on page 109 and, using the water-soluble pen or quilter's pencil, trace round and cut out two head pieces and eight limb pieces from the cream fleece, making sure the pile runs down the length of all the pieces. From the striped fleece, cut out two dress pieces, making sure the stripes run across the width of the dress. Remember to mark the position of the small dots.

2 Seam the neck edge of one of the dress pieces to the flat edge of the head, leaving a 5-mm (¼-in) seam allowance. Do the same with the second head and dress piece. Now seam up one side of the dress, round the head, and down the second side, again leaving a 5-mm (¼-in) seam allowance and leaving openings between the small dots for inserting the arms. Leave the lower edge of the dress open. Turn the body right sides out.

3 Place two of the limb pieces right sides together and pin or baste in position. Seam round the outside, leaving a 5-mm (¼-in) seam allowance and leaving the end open for turning and stuffing. Do the same with the other three limb pieces. Turn the limbs the right way out and stuff fairly lightly. Insert the arms through the holes in the sides of the body, tucking the raw edges of the dress inwards. Slip stitch in place using your thread double for extra strength. Now stuff the head and body.

4 Turn under 5 mm (¼ in) along the lower edge of the body and baste. Slip stitch the opening at the bottom of the dress closed, inserting the legs between the small dots and sewing them in as you go.

5 Cut out two outer eyes from pale blue felt and two inner eyes from black felt. Using the photograph as a guide, position the features and oversew them in place. When you have finished, gently tease around the stitches with the tip of a needle so that the stitches become almost invisible. With six strands of red embroidery thread, work the mouth in back stitch. For the eyelashes, work three small straight stitches at the outer edge of each eye, using three strands of black embroidery thread. For the hair, cut the grey fleece into strips along the length of the fabric. Starting at the forehead, 1.5 cm (¾ in) down from the centre seam of the head, back stitch the hair in place across the top and down the back of the head. You may find it helpful to draw your sewing line before you start using the water-soluble pen or quilter's pencil. Trim the hair at the back slightly to make it more even.

To make the hat and scarf

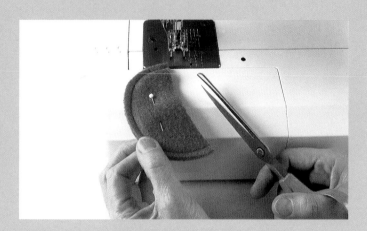

1 Photocopy the hat and flower templates on page 109 and cut them out. Use the template to cut out two hat pieces from the bright pink fleece, making sure that any obvious pile runs down the shorter length of the hat pieces. Place the two pieces right sides together and seam around the top curve of the hat leaving a 5-mm (¼-in) seam allowance. Trim the seam and turn the hat the right way out.

2 Using the water-soluble pen or quilter's pencil, draw round the flower template on the yellow felt and cut it out carefully. Using the photograph as a guide, position the flower on the hat and secure it in place by sewing on the red button for the flower centre. Finish the doll by tying a single knot in each end of the scarf and knotting it lightly around Mimi's neck.

To make Louis

1 Photocopy the puppy template on page 109 and cut it out. Use the template to cut out one dog shape, remembering to mark the position of the small dots, and making sure that any pile runs down the shape. Place the second piece of pale grey fleece face up on a hard, flat surface. Place the dog shape face down on this second piece of fleece and pin or baste in place.

2 Sew around the puppy, leaving a 5-mm (¼-in) seam allowance and leaving an opening between the two small dots for turning and stuffing. Trim the seam closely, turn the puppy the right way out, stuff lightly and close gap. Using three strands of black embroidery thread, work a French knot (see page 14) for Louis' eye on each side and a small embroidered nose. Use the red ribbon to make Louis' lead.

ANYA The Raggedy Anne

Anya is based on the traditional Raggedy Anne doll who starred in a story book published in 1918. Anya is a little different from the traditional dolls in that she's ditched the bloomers and traditional white pinafore in favour of an altogether more modern frock. But like the traditional dolls, she has a sweet and loving personality and wants to be everyone's friend.

You will need

MATERIALS
For the doll

- A piece of cream fleece, measuring 22 x 36 cm (8¾ x 14 in) (if the fabric has an obvious pile, this should run down the longer length of the fabric)
- A piece of striped fleece, measuring 20 x 15 cm (8 x 6 in) for the legs, with the stripe running across the longer length of the fleece
- A piece of black fleece, measuring 20 x 12 cm (8 x 4¾ in) for the boots (if the fabric has an obvious pile, this should run down the shorter length of the fabric)
- A small piece of orange fleece for the hair
- Scraps of mid-blue and black felt for the eyes
- A scrap of orange felt for the nose (or you could use a scrap of the orange fleece you are using for the hair)
- A scrap of mid-pink fleece or felt for the cheeks
- Black embroidery thread
- 30 g (1 oz) polyester toy filling
- Matching threads for all your fabrics, including the felt

Anya is approximately 34 cm (13½ in) tall

For the clothes

- Two pieces of floral cotton fabric, each measuring 17 x 15 cm (6¾ x 6 in) (if the pattern has an obvious direction, this should run down the longer length of the fabric)
- A piece of elastic cord for the neck of the dress, measuring approximately 16 cm (6¼ in)
- A 3-cm (12-in) length of ready-gathered broderie anglaise lace, approximately 4 cm (1½ in) deep
- Matching thread for your fabric

TOOLS

- Access to a photocopier
- Scissors
- Dressmaking pins
- Water-soluble pen or quilter's pencil
- Sewing machine (optional)
- Sewing needles
- Iron
- Small safety pin for threading the elastic cord

To make the doll

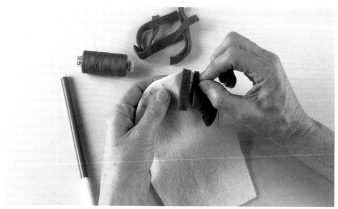

1 Photocopy the templates on page 110 and use them to cut out two head and body pieces and four arm pieces from the cream fleece and four boot pieces from the black fleece, making sure any obvious pile runs down the length of the pieces. Mark the position of the small dots and lines. Cut out four leg pieces from the striped fleece, making sure that the stripes run across the width of the pieces and the stripe pattern is identical on each leg piece.

2 Cut the orange fleece into nine strips, each measuring 1 x 8 cm (⅜ x 3¼ in). Fold each strip in half widthways and lay around the head of one of the head and body pieces in the position marked by the small lines. The loops should point inwards and the raw edges of the strips should line up with the raw edges of the head. Baste in place.

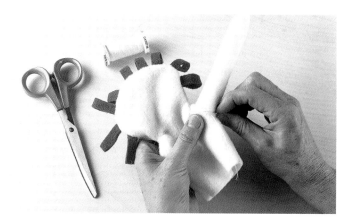

3 Fold the second head and body piece in half lengthwise, right sides together and sew the body dart – from the centre of the face into the neck, then from the neck outwards to the tummy. Place the two head and body pieces right sides together and seam round the outside, leaving a 5-mm (¼-in) seam allowance. Leave open at the bottom and between the two sets of small dots for inserting the arms. Turn right sides out.

4 Place two of the arm pieces right sides together and pin or baste in position. Seam round the outside, leaving a 5-mm (¼-in) seam allowance and leaving the end open for turning and stuffing. Do the same with the other two arm pieces. Turn the arms the right way out and stuff fairly lightly. Insert the arms through the holes in the sides of the body, tucking in the raw edges, and hand stitch in place using your thread double for extra strength.

5   Seam the top of the black boot pieces to the bottom of the leg pieces, allowing a 5-mm (¼-in) seam allowance. Now place two of the leg pieces right sides together. Seam round the outside, leaving a 5-mm (¼-in) seam allowance and leaving the top open for turning and stuffing. Do the same with the other two leg pieces. Turn the legs the right way out and stuff the boots firmly and the legs lightly.

6   To shape the boots, hold the leg so that the seams run down the front and back of the legs rather than the sides. Now turn up 4.5 cm (1¾ in) at the end of each boot and hold in place so that the foot of the boot is at a right angle to the leg. Using the thread double for strength and starting at one of the side seams, work a few large, loose slip stitches across the curve at the front of the ankle. Pull up the thread fairly tightly and secure.

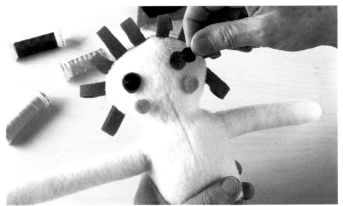

7   Stuff the head and body. Turn under 5 mm (¼ in) along the lower edge of the body and baste. Insert the top of the legs into the body so that the edge of the legs line up with the sides of the body. Slip stitch in place using your thread double for extra strength and slip stitch across the crotch.

8   Cut out two outer eyes from mid-blue felt, two inner eyes from black felt, two cheeks from the pink fleece (or felt) and the nose from orange felt (or fleece). Using the photograph as a guide, position the features and oversew them in place. With three strands of black embroidery thread, work the mouth in back stitch. Work single stitches for the lower eyelashes and eyebrows. Tie a bow in Anya's hair.

To make the dress

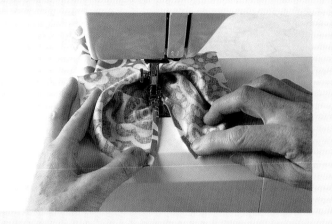

1 Lay the two rectangles of fabric right sides together. (If your fabric has an obvious direction, make sure it is the right way up.) Measure down 7.5 cm (3 in) from the top of the fabric on each of the longer sides and make a small mark with the water-soluble pen or quilter's pencil to mark the bottom of the armholes. Seam down each side from the armhole mark to the bottom of the dress, leaving a 5-mm (¼-in) seam allowance.

2 Press under 5 mm (¼ in) on each side of the two armholes and press open the side seams using the iron. If you are using a sewing machine, work a small zig zag stitch down the raw edges on both sides of the armholes. If you are hand stitching, tuck under the raw edge of the armholes and slip stitch in place.

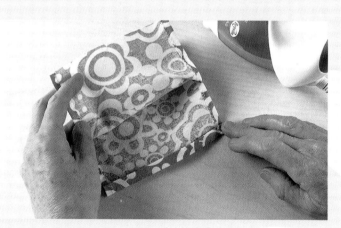

3 Press under 5 mm (¼ in) along the top edges of both sides of the dress. Press under another 5 mm (¼ in) to form a casing and stitch very close to the folded edge. Using the small safety pin, thread the elastic through the casing. Pull up the elastic quite tightly (so the neck of the dress is about the same width as the doll's neck) and knot the ends together tightly. Trim the knot ends and conceal the knot in the casing.

4 Press under 5 mm (¼ in) along the bottom edge of the dress. Press under another 5 mm (¼ in) and stitch close to the folded edge. Press under 5 mm (¼ in) along the edge of the beginning of the lace. Starting at the back of the dress, baste the lace along the lower edge of the dress, so the top edge of the lace is on the underside of the dress. When you get to the beginning point, trim the lace and press under the raw edge. Stitch in place and slip stitch the pressed edges together.

Templates

All templates are shown at 50% of actual size and will need to be enlarged to 100% using a photocopier before use.

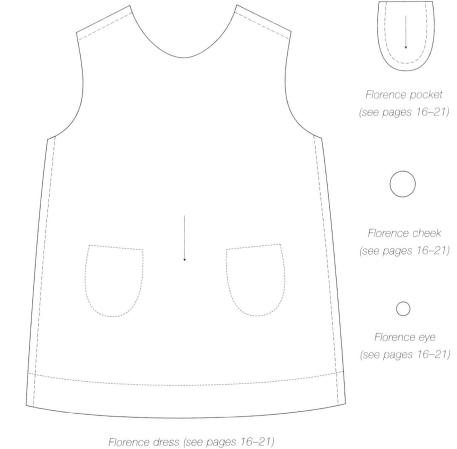

Florence dress (see pages 16–21)

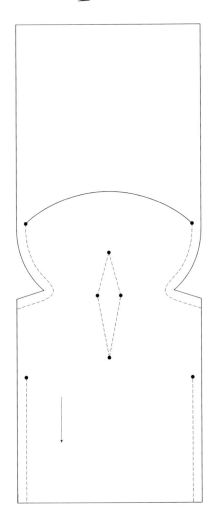

Florence head and body (see pages 16–21)

Florence pocket
(see pages 16–21)

Florence cheek
(see pages 16–21)

Florence eye
(see pages 16–21)

Florence arm (see pages 16–21)

Florence shoe (see pages 16–21)

Florence leg (see pages 16–21)

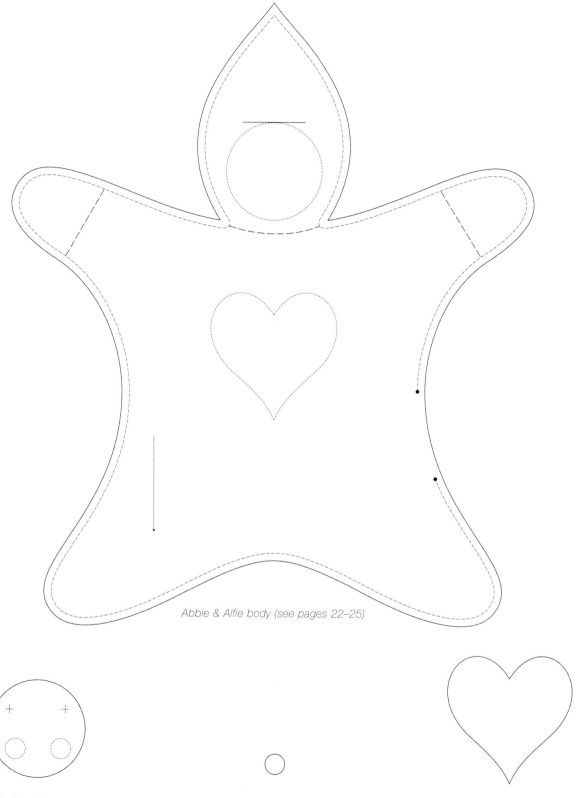

Abbie & Alfie body (see pages 22–25)

Abbie & Alfie face (see pages 22–25)

Abbie & Alfie cheek (see pages 22–25)

Abbie & Alfie heart (see pages 22–25)

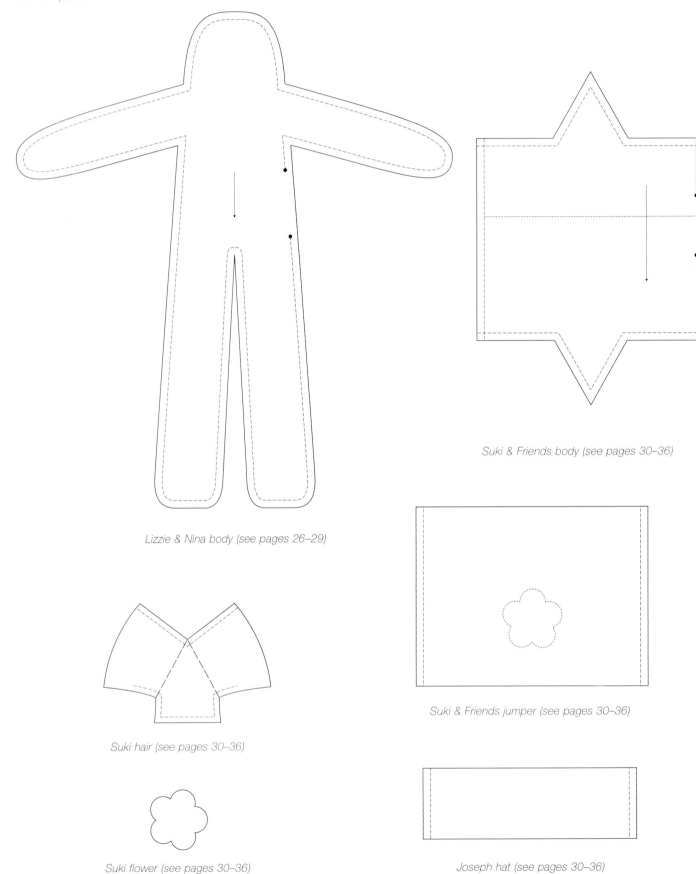

Lizzie & Nina body (see pages 26–29)

Suki & Friends body (see pages 30–36)

Suki hair (see pages 30–36)

Suki & Friends jumper (see pages 30–36)

Suki flower (see pages 30–36)

Joseph hat (see pages 30–36)

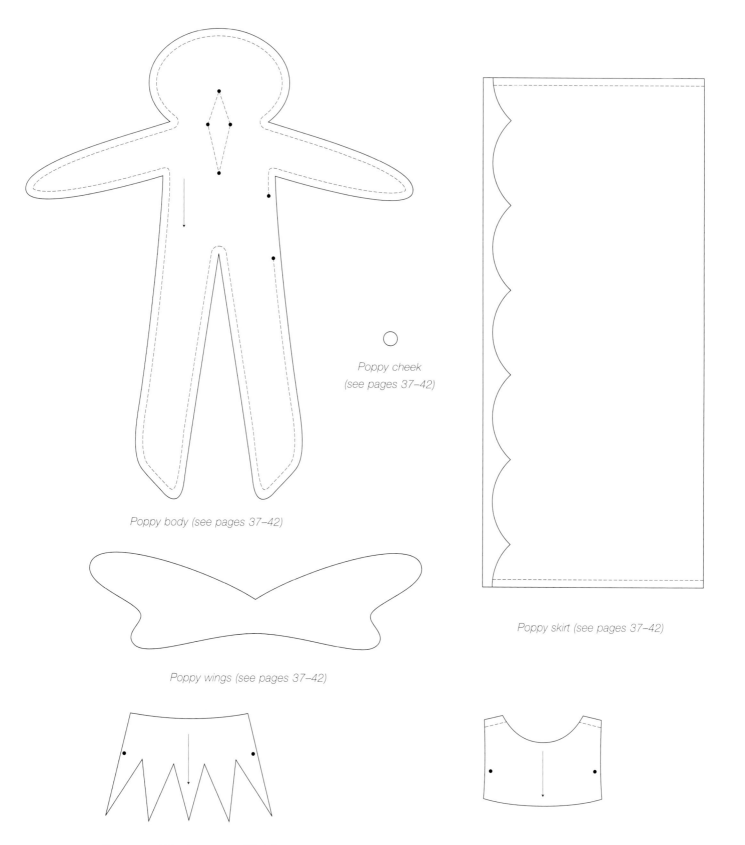

Poppy body (see pages 37–42)

Poppy cheek
(see pages 37–42)

Poppy skirt (see pages 37–42)

Poppy wings (see pages 37–42)

Poppy sepal trim (see pages 37–42)

Poppy bodice (see pages 37–42)

Olga body back (see pages 43–47)

Olga body front (see pages 43–47)

Daisy bonnet front (see pages 48–54)

Daisy face (see pages 48–54)

Olga flower (see pages 43–47)

Olga hair (see pages 43–47)

Daisy smock bodice (see pages 48–54)

Olga flower centre (see pages 43–47)

Olga face (see pages 43–47)

Olga cheek (see pages 43–47)

Daisy bonnet back (see pages 48–54)

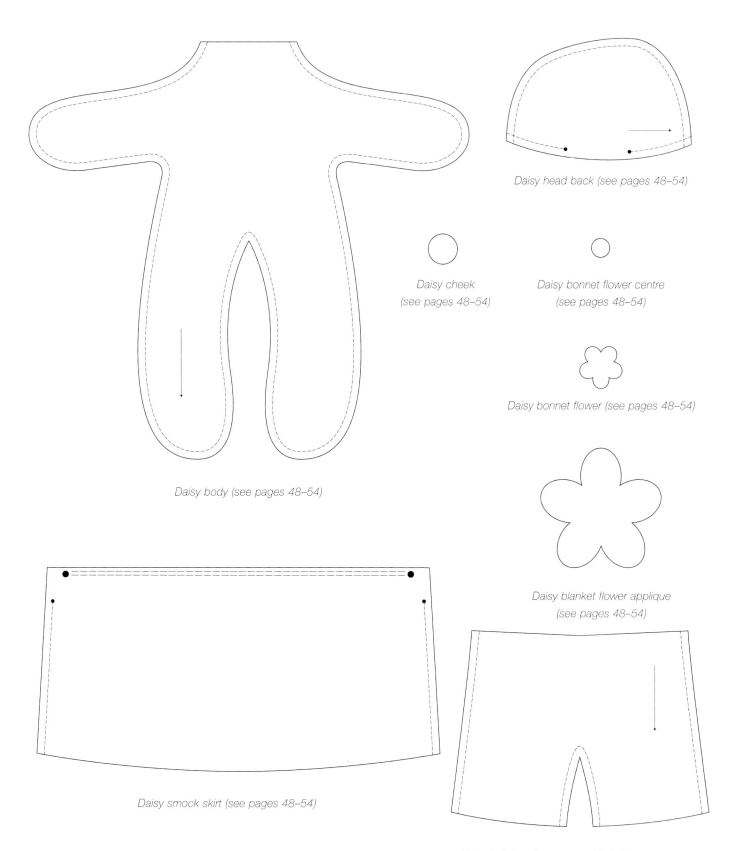

Daisy head back (see pages 48–54)

Daisy cheek
(see pages 48–54)

Daisy bonnet flower centre
(see pages 48–54)

Daisy bonnet flower (see pages 48–54)

Daisy body (see pages 48–54)

Daisy blanket flower applique
(see pages 48–54)

Daisy smock skirt (see pages 48–54)

Daisy knickers (see pages 48–54)

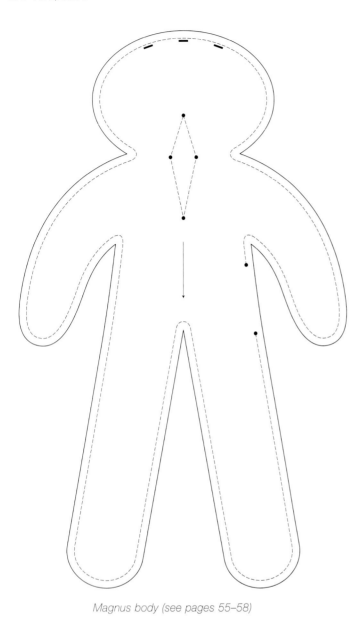

Magnus body (see pages 55–58)

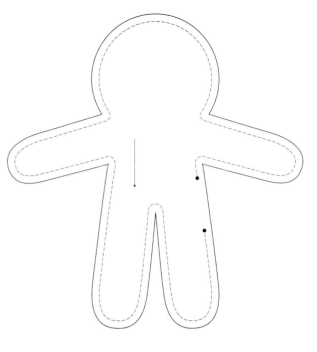

Ruby & Zak body (see pages 59–63)

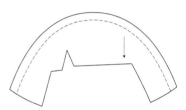

Ruby hair front (see pages 59–63)

Magnus inner eyes (see pages 55–58)

*Magnus mid-layer of smaller eye
(see pages 55–58)*

Ruby dress (see pages 59–63)

*Magnus outer of larger eye
(see pages 55–58)*

*Magnus outer of smaller eye and mid-layer
of larger eye (see pages 55–58)*

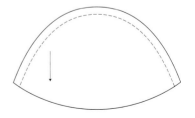

Ruby hair back (see pages 59–63)

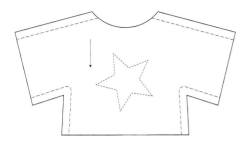

Zak jumper (see pages 59–63)

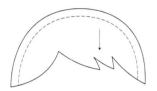

Zak hair front (see pages 59–63)

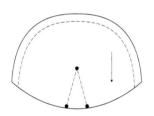

Zak hair back (see pages 59–63)

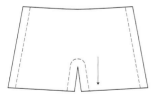

Zak shorts (see pages 59–63)

Zak star (see pages 59–63)

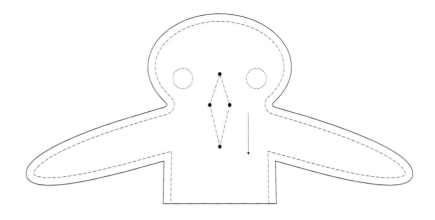

Tilly body (see pages 64–68)

Tilly cheek (see pages 64–68)

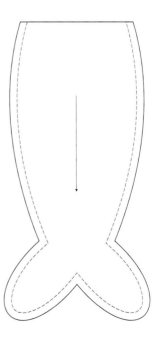

Tilly tail (see pages 64–68)

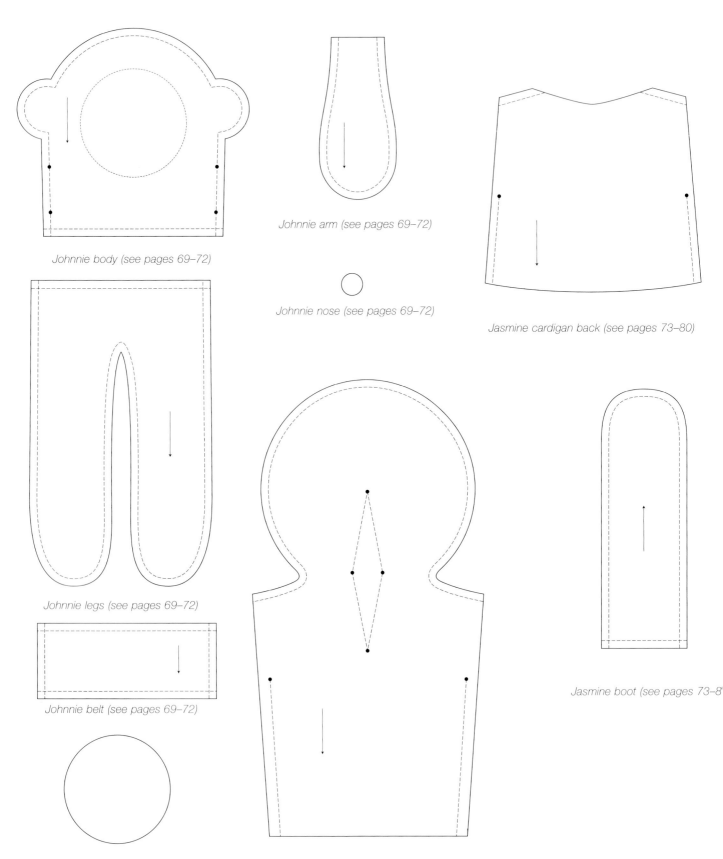

Johnnie body (see pages 69–72)

Johnnie arm (see pages 69–72)

Johnnie nose (see pages 69–72)

Jasmine cardigan back (see pages 73–80)

Johnnie legs (see pages 69–72)

Jasmine boot (see pages 73–8)

Johnnie belt (see pages 69–72)

Johnnie face (see pages 69–72)

Jasmine head and body (see pages 73–80)

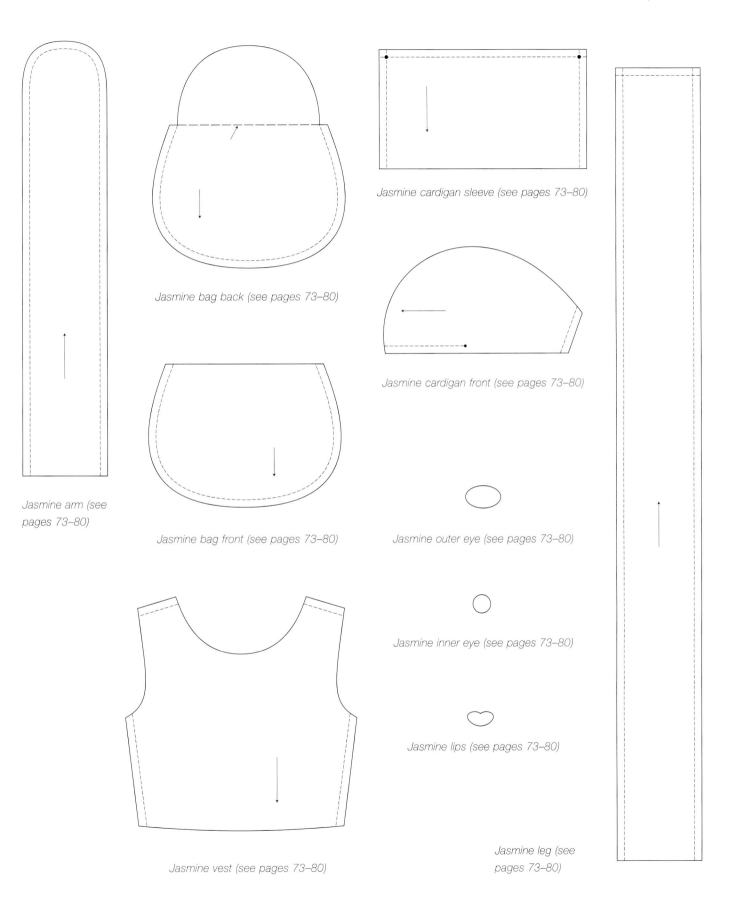

Jasmine arm (see pages 73–80)

Jasmine bag back (see pages 73–80)

Jasmine bag front (see pages 73–80)

Jasmine cardigan sleeve (see pages 73–80)

Jasmine cardigan front (see pages 73–80)

Jasmine outer eye (see pages 73–80)

Jasmine inner eye (see pages 73–80)

Jasmine lips (see pages 73–80)

Jasmine vest (see pages 73–80)

Jasmine leg (see pages 73–80)

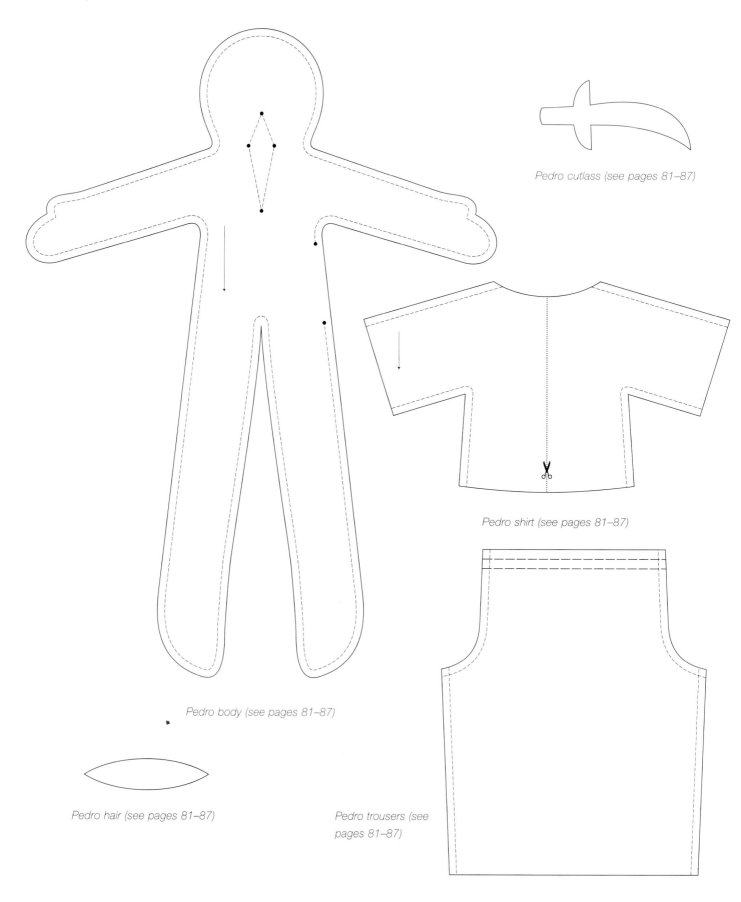

Pedro cutlass (see pages 81–87)

Pedro shirt (see pages 81–87)

Pedro body (see pages 81–87)

Pedro hair (see pages 81–87)

Pedro trousers (see pages 81–87)

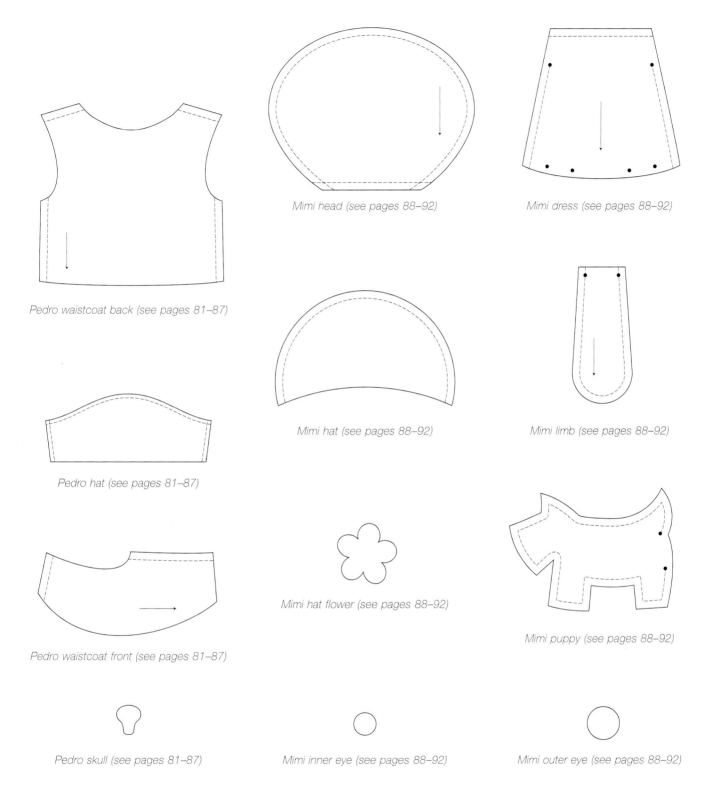

Pedro waistcoat back (see pages 81–87)

Mimi head (see pages 88–92)

Mimi dress (see pages 88–92)

Pedro hat (see pages 81–87)

Mimi hat (see pages 88–92)

Mimi limb (see pages 88–92)

Mimi hat flower (see pages 88–92)

Mimi puppy (see pages 88–92)

Pedro waistcoat front (see pages 81–87)

Pedro skull (see pages 81–87)

Mimi inner eye (see pages 88–92)

Mimi outer eye (see pages 88–92)

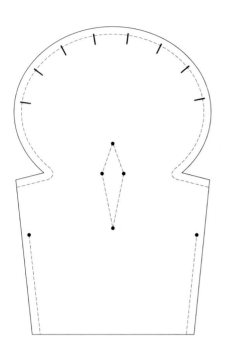

Anya head and body (see pages 93–97)

Anya leg (see pages 93–97)

Anya arm (see pages 93–97)

Anya inner eye (see pages 93–97)

Anya nose (see pages 93–97)

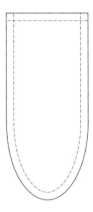

Anya boot (see pages 93–97)

Anya outer eye (see pages 93–97)

Anya cheek (see pages 93–97)

Suppliers

MAIL ORDER AND INTERNET SUPPLIERS

FABRIC LAND
Telephone 01425 461444
Email sue.fabricland@tiscali.co.uk
Website www.fabricland.co.uk
Fabric (including fleece) and haberdashery. Telephone orders and internet orders accepted. Fabric Land also has 11 retail branches throughout the south of England.

FABRIC UK
Registered office:
Carlton Business Centre
Saltley Road
Birmingham B7 4TH
Telephone 0870 350 1936
Email kbt@fabricuk.com
Website www.fabricuk.com
Fabric (including fleece) and haberdashery. Telephone orders and internet orders accepted.

PLANET FLEECE
21A Whitehorse Street
Baldock
Hertfordshire SG7 6QB
Telephone 01462 491500
Email sewing@planetfleece.co.uk
Website www.planetfleece.co.uk
Fleece and haberdashery. Mostly internet orders. Telephone before visiting.

THE COTTON PATCH
1283–1285 Stratford Road
Hall Green
Birmingham B28 9AJ
Telephone 0121 702 2840
Email mailorder@cottonpatch.co.uk
Website www.cottonpatch.co.uk
Wide range of patchwork fabrics and haberdashery items.

RETAIL OUTLETS

BOROVIK FABRICS
16 Berwick Street
London W1F 0HP
Telephone 020 7437 2180
Wide range of fabrics including fleece, cottons and speciality fabrics, available at the shop only.

FABRIC WAREHOUSE LTD
Packet Boat Lane
Uxbridge
Middlesex UB8 2JP
Telephone 01895 448465
Email enquiries@thefabricwarehouse.com
Website www.thefabricwarehouseltd.com
Wide range of fleece and other fabrics, and haberdashery items available at the shop only.

HOBBYCRAFT GROUP LTD
Telephone 0800 027 2387 for details of local stores
Website www.hobbycraft.co.uk
28 stores in England and Wales with wide range of haberdashery items, knitting wools and patchwork fabrics. Call for details of your nearest store or see website.

JOHN LEWIS PARTNERSHIP
Head Office:
Partnership House
Carlisle Place
London SW1P 1BX
Telephone 020 7828 1000
Website www.johnlewis.com
Haberdashery and knitting wools. Some stores also sell fabrics. Stores throughout England and Scotland. Phone for details of your local store or look on the website.

Index